SHERLOCK

THE CASEBOOK

GUY ADAMS

BOOKS

THE ADVENTURE OF THE REBORN DETECTIVE

Say what you like about trains – and folk do, they split opinion awfully – but people have good ideas on them. Perhaps the brain just responds well to lousy tea and slow forward momentum. When the idea for *Sherlock* was born, the train in question was running between Cardiff and London, and the gently propelled brains doing the heavy lifting belonged to Steven Moffat and Mark Gatiss.

Steven Moffat

They were travelling to and from the *Doctor Who* production office, a show they have a considerable history with. Both had contributed scripts for the programme. Mark had also starred in one, starting off as an elderly scientist before rejuvenating then mutating and finally getting slapped all over Southwark Cathedral. In 2009, determined not to be outdone by such theatrics, Steven took over as executive producer and lead writer for the show, with Mark continuing to contribute scripts since. All of this involved a good number of train journeys.

And thinking.

Mark Gatiss

And good ideas.

The idea of reinventing Sir Arthur Conan Doyle's Sherlock Holmes as a modern-day detective began as little more than a mental exercise.

'We kept talking about things that we would like to do,' says Mark, 'and Sherlock Holmes came up again and again.'

But not just any Sherlock Holmes – a Sherlock Holmes lifted out of history and set right at the heart of the present day.

'It came down to the fact that we secretly liked the Rathbones best,' continues Mark, referring to the series of Sherlock Holmes films produced between 1939 and 1946 starring Basil Rathbone as Holmes, 'particularly the ones where they brought them up to date. [See 'The Adventure of the Differing Deerstalkers', p.138 for more about Rathbone as Holmes.] These cheeky B-movies seemed to us to be closer to Doyle than almost any other version. Perhaps because his own attitude towards his creation was so casual that somehow these potboilers really got it.'

Many screen adaptations of Doyle's adventures have been incredibly serious and reverent, and while that might be understandable when dealing with something so highly regarded it can also limit the scope of those adaptations. Good ideas and great characters should be revelled in, not slavishly reproduced.

Despite the appeal of reworking Holmes, it took Steven and Mark a long time to consider developing it as a series. Eventually it was through the involvement and encouragement of Sue Vertue, Steven's wife and producer at Hartswood Films, that it became something they actively pursued rather than just something with which to while away a long journey.

'I mentioned it to Sue not even as a pitch, just in conversation,' says Steven. '"We keep talking about this," I said, "and one day someone's going to do it and we're going to be so cross." To which she sensibly replied, "Well, you do it then."'

'It's not as if we were on this train heading to a sales conference or something,' says Mark. 'We were both working on the biggest show on television! And yet it didn't occur to us that maybe we could actually make *Sherlock*! We could have made it several years earlier than we did, because we talked about it for ages.'

Steven agrees. 'We both had very good careers – if we'd gone in and pitched it, we'd have been fine. There was nothing to stop us. You just don't know if it's a private delusion, do you?'

Was there really a place for a modern-day Sherlock Holmes? Where would he fit in a TV landscape already littered with cop shows?

'Exactly,' says Steven. 'Doyle effectively created the CSI, forensic procedural format with the character of Holmes. So what would make him stand out, now that his methods are more commonplace? In the end, it came down to a simple fact: he would still be the cleverest man in the room. He would still be a genius.'

So, with Sue Vertue thinking it was a good idea…

'We didn't talk to anyone who *didn't* think it was a good idea…' Steven points out, 'but it was interesting that she liked it, because I didn't *expect* her to. That was the first clue to the fact that this was a big hit. This woman who had never read Sherlock Holmes, who had no interest in Sherlock Holmes in fact, saying

Another contemporary Holmes – Basil Rathbone

"That's a really good idea." She nagged us and got us to sit down and get on with it.'

In Monte Carlo, no less.

'That's a story that got out of control!' laughs Mark. 'I saw someone saying that the BBC flew us to Monte Carlo to develop the show, but we were there anyway, attending an awards ceremony.'

'If you have to do it somewhere, though…' suggests Steven.

Certainly, the idyllic scenery of Monaco must have certain advantages over a grimy window on the 9.45 to Cardiff Central. The food's nicer, too.

'Oh, it was lovely,' Mark agrees, 'and the ideas began tumbling over each other.'

'A lot of what we were doing,' explains Steven, 'was thinking about what it felt like when you were a kid first reading those stories. When I first read them I wasn't thinking, "Oh, this is all very Victorian." I was thinking, "How does he do all these deductions?" And I do remember the genuine sense of shock when I read *A Study in Scarlet* – which I did read first, I'm one of the few people to have read Sherlock Holmes in the right order – realising how unpleasant Holmes is! I had always thought that Sherlock Holmes would be like

James Bond; he would be strong and brave and wise. But he wasn't – he was *horrible*, and he did all sorts of weird things, and then he started taking drugs, and I was: "Oh my goodness, this is shocking!"'

'It's all there,' adds Mark. 'There are whole tracts of these stories that have never been touched by other adaptations, some of the most famous highlights of sensational literature, the most wonderful facets of Holmes's character... The Doyle story of *The Five Orange Pips*, for example. The story wouldn't work today [it hinges on the reader not knowing that KKK stands for Ku Klux Klan], but the idea of getting these five orange pips through the post is wonderful, it's spooky. And what about *The Adventure of Black Peter*? It's not a very good story, really, but it starts with Holmes coming in carrying a harpoon having spent the morning spearing pigs! Why not?'

Why not indeed? The opening is, of course, duplicated in Mark's episode *The Hounds of Baskerville*, one of many references, explicit or veiled, to the original stories contained in the show.

'We just love it so much,' admits Steven, as if we could be in any doubt. 'And sometimes those references are there as a joke, just for fun, or sometimes they're there because the ideas are simply good and untouched, waiting for someone to use them. These stories are brilliant! The idea that Doyle had of coming up with the unrecorded cases, mentioning things you've never seen – brilliant! It's something we've got used to, but it's brilliant. The one thing we can't quite capture is the innovation of those ideas, how incredibly clever they were. And the idea that Holmes starts reviewing, negatively, the stories he's in! That's a mind-expanding idea that we've just got used to. The fact that he looks at something we've just enjoyed and says, "That was terrible."'

An opinion that places Sherlock Holmes firmly in the minority, when it comes to the original stories and to their new lease of life in Sherlock. Still, the fact that Doyle's original stories remain so popular today rather proves how good they are. They are tales that have never gone out of fashion, and Sherlock Holmes and Doctor Watson have become characters utterly embedded in the world's consciousness. One only has to visit the Holmes museum on Baker Street. Once you've circumnavigated the slightly bored doorman and – on the day I visited, anyway – the extremely Polish Sherlock Holmes loitering in his faux study, straightening his pipes, you will find a folder of letters sent from all over the world by people believing Sherlock Holmes to be real. For a period of time, the bank whose Baker Street office swallowed up the fictional address of 221B employed a secretary specifically to handle the non-existent detective's correspondence. While both Doyle and his hero dismissed the value of the Holmes stories, history has refused to agree with them. It may be difficult to second-guess the public's taste, and good fortune plays a hand, but there's a reason why we're not all as familiar with other turn-of-the century heroes. Inspector Lipinski? Hagar Stanley, the gypsy detective? Horace Dorrington? Surely you remember Lady Molly of Scotland Yard?

221B Baker Street (actually North Gower Street)

No, to still be loved after all these years takes something rather extraordinary.

And loved the idea still was. Given the go-ahead by the BBC to develop the show, Hartswood Films produced a pilot episode, *A Study in Pink*, that was designed to introduce the revised characters and the modern world they inhabited. Newspapers and websites reported on the planned series, announcing that the pilot episode was to be broadcast in the autumn of 2009 with a series to be broadcast at a later date should the show be sufficiently popular.

'Everything that matters about Holmes and Watson is the same,' announced Steven Moffat in the press release. 'Conan Doyle's original stories were never about frock coats and gas light. They're about brilliant detection, dreadful villains and blood-curdling crimes – and, frankly, the hell with the crinoline.'

'Other detectives have cases, Sherlock Holmes has adventures and that's what matters.'

So Sherlock's first new adventure was about to begin. But who was to play the iconic detective?

'Benedict Cumberbatch was our first and only choice,' says Mark, 'so it was just down to finding our Watson, which didn't take us that long…'

'We saw a lot of very good people,' adds Steven, 'but our view of who was good changed once Benedict was on board, because then it had to be about who would work well with him. When Benedict stood next to Martin Freeman and they started to do their thing, we just said, "That's it! That's what we need." They looked right together.'

'With the others,' continues Mark, 'the chemistry either wasn't there or it was different. With one actor you had a real sense of Watson as a military man, but he was more of a sergeant than a doctor. He would be faithful to Sherlock, a real rock of reliability, which is important with the character, but the status between them was wrong. Then there were a couple of others that were just too dominant – you had two alpha males, two Sherlocks!'

The greatest strength of the Sherlock Holmes stories is the great friendship that lies at the heart of them. Finding the two actors that would bring that friendship to life was a major battle won. Still, there was another character detail to address, one that feels trivial and silly in hindsight but momentous at the time.

'What do they call each other?' asks Steven. 'It was immediately obvious they couldn't refer to each other by their surnames.'

It had always been Holmes and Watson, in the stories; the idea of 'Sherlock' and 'John' at first feels against the grain.

'It takes a lot of getting used to,' Steven agrees, 'but the alternative would have been awful. It would have made them sound like public schoolboys, it would have made them sound boorish.'

With their central characters in place, casting continued and the production of the pilot gathered pace.

Shooting was predominantly planned to take place in Cardiff, albeit with a few days in London to take advantage of some of the more iconic locations the capital offered. Not least of all of these would be Sherlock and John's flat, 221B Baker Street, an address as famous as the fictional characters who lived

Behind the scenes on the first episode

The new 'movie-length' format allowed for extra scenes that wouldn't have been in the hour-long series

there. But how to represent their home in this new, modern version?

'It would have been wrong to put him in a block of flats,' says Steven, 'because there aren't any there. It would have felt stupid and contrived. It had to be Baker Street still, but Baker Street as it is now.'

It was also agreed that the flat number had to be plainly visible (however unlikely it would be to have an upstairs flat advertised on the front door. 221? Yes. 221B? Not so much...) So the front door, heavy and black with the iconic number plainly visible at its centre remains the entrance to Sherlock and John's world. Though it's not actually on Baker Street.

'We briefly considered using the real Baker Street,' says Mark, 'and it would have been possible, but it's such a busy road and just the task of covering the thousands of things with "Sherlock Holmes" written on them would have made it impossible.' In reality, the show films on North Gower Street, half a mile or so away, a much more practical alternative.

The pilot was shot and delivered to the BBC. Soon afterwards came the announcement that Sherlock had been commissioned as a series of three 90-minute episodes. The unscreened pilot would later be included as a special feature on the DVD and Blu-ray releases of Series One; in the meantime, Steven and Mark suddenly found themselves with the chance to rethink certain elements of the show.

'Doing a pilot gives you the opportunity to change your mind about some of the small things,' Mark points out, 'and to correct things that worked on paper but not on the screen.'

This was no longer a six-episode run of hour-long stories, it was a run of three full-length movies. Was the change a good thing?

'I think this is better, yes,' says Steven. 'Tonally the show would have been the same, but you wouldn't have had a lot of things we've been able to do with the longer episodes. You would never have had Christmas in Baker Street!'

'It's all about scale,' Mark agrees. 'One of the cases in [third episode] *The Great Game* originally took up a whole episode, but when you think in terms of writing these movies – when you ask "How brilliant it would be if Sherlock were able to solve that in fifteen minutes not an hour?" – that's what gives you this fantastic sense of scale.'

And, on 25 July 2010, an eager public was able to judge for itself as the first episode, *A Study in Pink* was broadcast on BBC One... ∎

A Study in Pink

You're keeping A SCRAPBOOK.

Only old ladies and pre-pubescent girls keep scrapbooks, John.

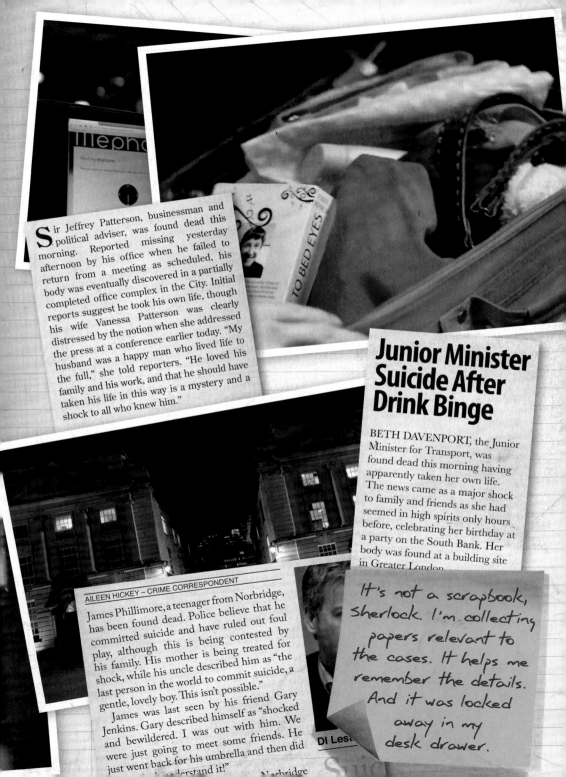

Sir Jeffrey Patterson, businessman and political adviser, was found dead this morning. Reported missing yesterday afternoon by his office when he failed to return from a meeting as scheduled, his body was eventually discovered in a partially completed office complex in the City. Initial reports suggest he took his own life, though his wife Vanessa Patterson was clearly distressed by the notion when she addressed the press at a conference earlier today. "My husband was a happy man who lived life to the full," she told reporters. "He loved his family and his work, and that he should have taken his life in this way is a mystery and a shock to all who knew him."

Junior Minister Suicide After Drink Binge

BETH DAVENPORT, the Junior Minister for Transport, was found dead this morning having apparently taken her own life. The news came as a major shock to family and friends as she had seemed in high spirits only hours before, celebrating her birthday at a party on the South Bank. Her body was found at a building site in Greater London.

AILEEN HICKEY – CRIME CORRESPONDENT

James Phillimore, a teenager from Norbridge, has been found dead. Police believe that he committed suicide and have ruled out foul play, although this is being contested by his family. His mother is being treated for shock, while his uncle described him as "the last person in the world to commit suicide, a gentle, lovely boy. This isn't possible."

James was last seen by his friend Gary Jenkins. Gary described himself as "shocked and bewildered. I was out with him. We were just going to meet some friends. He just went back for his umbrella and then did ... understand it!"

DI Lest...   Norbridge

It's not a scrapbook, Sherlock. I'm collecting papers relevant to the cases. It helps me remember the details. And it was locked away in my desk drawer.

A study in Pink

The lock on your desk drawer was insulting me with its pretence at security. IT'S A SCRAPBOOK. And if you ordered your mind properly you wouldn't need it to help you remember things.

I presume my ties were insulting you too? I had to put them away twice yesterday.

My mind is perfectly ordered.

This morning, DI Greg Lestrade held a press conference in relation to the death of Junior Transport Minister Beth Davenport. It was confirmed by Sergeant Sally Donovan, part of the investigation team, that "this apparent suicide closely resembles those of Sir Jeffery Patterson and James Phillimore. In light of this, these incidents are now being treated as linked."

Sergeant Donovan clarified that while the investigation was ongoing, DI Lestrade would take questions from reporters in attendance. Despite this promise, her superior seemed singularly obstructive and uninformative. When asked how suicides could be linked, it was explained that "they had all taken the same poison. They were all found in places they had no reason to be and none of them had shown a previous inclination towards suicide." One of the reporters was happy to share his incredulity, insisting that you could not have serial suicides. To which Lestrade unhelpfully replied "Well, apparently you can."

He further went on to inspire scant confidence when asked whether there was a link between the three deceased. "There's no link we've found yet," he said, "but there has to be one." At which point, in a truly bizarre twist of events, all those attending received a text message from an undisclosed sender. That message contained only one word but was clear in its opinion of DI Lestrade. "Wrong," it said. Clearly flustered by this, both Sergeant Donovan and DI Lestrade asked the reporters to ignore the text.

Attempting to bring the press conference to an end, DI Lestrade announced that the suicides were clearly linked and that they had their best officers investigating. At which point our mysterious text-messager repeated his previous contribution.

More out of control than ever, Lestrade asked for one final question. When asked whether there was any chance that these apparent suicides were in fact murders, he insisted that "The poison was clearly self-administered." He was asked how the public were to keep safe and, in a moment of crass insensitivity that shows the police force in general and DI Lestrade in particular as the blundering, crass and useless bodies they are, his response to the well-intentioned enquiry was simply "Don't commit suicide." ●

"DON'T COMMIT SUICIDE!"

TODAY OUR NATION'S police force hit a new low in intelligence and sensitivity.

Representatives of the national press gathered this morning to listen to the insipid offerings of DI Greg Lestrade, an officer already well known for his lax work in relation to the Hoey case last year. Talking now on the recent spate of alleged 'serial suicides' he could barely string a reassuring sentence together and concluded with his, by now extensively reported, suggestion that if the public wanted to stay safe then "Don't commit suicide." One might be tempted to offer him the same advice with regard to what he laughingly calls his career. Though one suspects it's far too late for that.

Your mind is cluttered with useless information. I was arranging your ties according to their dominant colour. **LEAVE THEM ALONE.**

As I made clear yesterday, remembering your clothes sizes is not 'useless information'.

Clothes either fit or they don't, what's the point in retaining all those numbers and letters?

A Study in Pink

Jenifer Wilson, body found by kids at an abandoned house, 3 Lauriston Gardens.

Scratched into the wood with the nails of her left hand, the message 'Rache'. Anderson suggested it might be the German word 'rache' meaning 'revenge'. Sherlock disagreed - more likely she had been trying to write the name 'Rachel'. The fact that she used her left hand to do so means she must be left-handed.

All jewellery clean except for her wedding ring which was dirty on the outside but polished on the inside. The ring was at least ten years old. Sherlock concluded that she had been unhappily married for most of that time and frequently had affairs. She took pride in her jewellery but couldn't bring herself to clean the wedding band because it meant so little to her. Frequent removal had ensured it stayed shiny on the inside.

Given her dress, she was clearly a professional woman, Sherlock guessed at a job in the media based on the 'alarming' shade of pink.

Splash marks on her right ankle and calf showed that she had been pulling along a wheeled suitcase. This case was nowhere to be found.

Oh God - a scrapbook with pictures of dead people in it.

I'm sure your counsellor would approve. You realise what this says about you?

Her coat was damp, across the back and under the collar. She had been walking in rain, collar turned up. Umbrella in her pocket still dry. Wherever she was it must have been too windy to use it.

This from the man who keeps an alphabetised collection of dog hair in the bathroom.

Given that the coat was still damp she couldn't have travelled for more than two or three hours. Checking within the radius of travel that time allowed, only Cardiff had had the sort of strong wind and rain that fitted the facts.

No case was found near the body, the killer's first mistake. Until then there was no evidence to prove the victims hadn't been alone when they died. Jennifer Wilson's case had been taken by the murderer.

A Study in Pink

Date: 28/01/10

Case No: 1878

Forensic Officer: S. Anderson

Subject: Sir Jeffrey Patterson

- **Age:** 52
  Hair: Light blond/grey
  Weight: 102kg

- **POISONING:** External sign of poisoning is limited, the skin tone and lips appearing normal within the parameters of coagulation and de-oxygenation. A sharp, citrus smell was present around the mouth. On opening the abdomen, the smell was far more distinct, positively pronounced when cutting open the stomach. Either the poison is slow to break down or the food present helped retard the process. The victim had eaten several rounds of coronation chicken sandwiches (white focaccia bread and heavy on the coriander) shortly before ingesting the poison and carbohydrates have been known to slow down the metabolisation of chemicals ...the praxis range.

Stolen police paperwork? There's hope for you yet.

Though anything written by Anderson is questionable. He is the prose equivalent of white noise.

He speaks highly of you too.

Apparently you're the only person he'd perform a post mortem on in his own time.

If his scalpel is as sharp as his intellect he can name the date.

Jennifer Wilson —

07689 154 301

Sherlock was sure that the murderer would only have kept Jennifer Wilson's suitcase by accident. The only way they could have done that is if they had driven her to Lauriston Gardens and the case had been left in the car. Equally, as soon as they had discovered their mistake, they would abandon the case. He found it — the same alarming shade of pink, naturally — in a skip not far from the house.

Jennifer Wilson's phone was missing, it must have been left in the car as well as the case. And now the murderer had it. And Sherlock had just had me send a text from my phone. Wonderful.

TO: +44772057747

What happened at Lauriston Gdns? I must have blacked out. 22 Northumberland St. Please come.

Which shows how much I like you, I wouldn't have let just anyone do it.

It's fascinating to see you lay all this out. Everything mentioned so far should be the equivalent of a moment's thought

and yet it's taken you pages to spell it all out. It's like listening to music that's been slowed down to a tenth of its proper speed.

This is what it's like with a normal brain, it's a wonder we get by.

A Study in Pink

We waited at Angelo's, across from 22 Northumberland Street.

After a while, Sherlock spotted a cab loitering outside the address. He decided we should give chase.

It was a dead end. Nothing gained but a scared American tourist and a stitch.

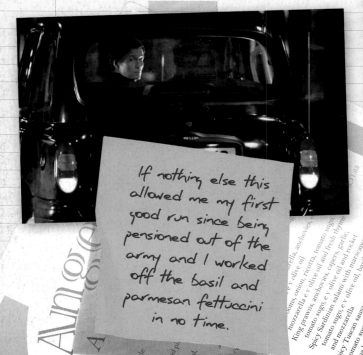

If nothing else this allowed me my first good run since being pensioned out of the army and I worked off the basil and parmesan fettuccini in no time.

Really?
By my estimation you've been gaining around a pound a week in weight. But then if you will eat all the time...

That said, a fun lit... I haven't l... so much the cas... the Blet... Poison...

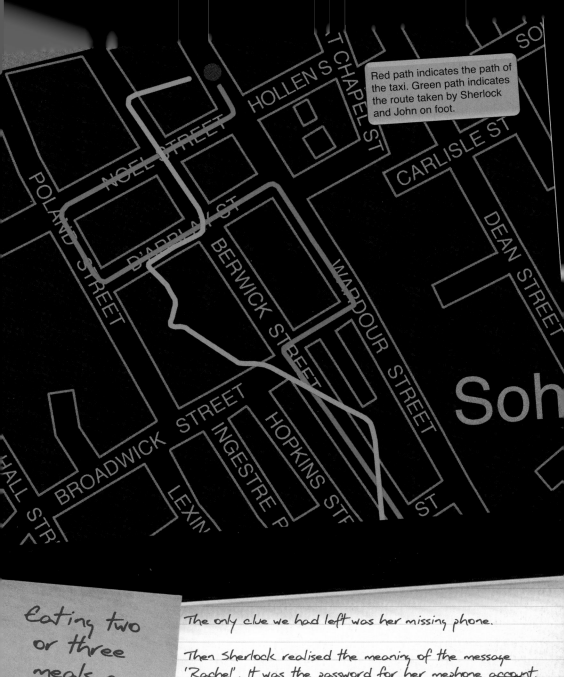

Red path indicates the path of the taxi. Green path indicates the route taken by Sherlock and John on foot.

Eating two or three meals a day is not 'all the time'.

The only clue we had left was her missing phone.

Then Sherlock realised the meaning of the message 'Rachel'. It was the password for her mephone account. She hadn't lost the phone, she'd planted it deliberately. Trace the phone and we could trace the killer!

It never occurred to us that he might want to trace us first...

A study in Pink

'Who do we trust even if we don't know them?' asked Sherlock. Taxi driver Jeff Hope provided the answer.

Having traced Sherlock, he drew him away by promising the one thing the silly git could never refuse: an answer.

The method was simple and enforced at gunpoint. Two pills: one poison, one not. The victim has the choice, they take one and Hope takes the other. But would they choose correctly?

I'd have come up with the answer myself soon enough.

+44772057747
160/1 of 6
COME WITH ME

We'll never know will we?

CAPITAL CA

HACKNEY CARRIAGE & PRIVATE HIRE DRIVER

Licence No. 91197

Licence No.
Jeff Hope

Expiry Date: 20/10/2012

MYSTERY SHOOTING AT FURTHER EDUCATION COLLEGE

Yesterday, North London residents were shocked by a shooting at the Roland-Kerr Further Education College. Though details are still vague it is known that the gunshot victim was Jeff Hope, a taxi driver.

The shooting took place at just after one in the morning within the college itself. The identity of the gunman is unknown as is that of another man photographed at the scene who appeared to have been suffering from shock.

Police were quick to respond to the situation. Spotted at the scene was DI Lestrade, famous for his role in the recent 'Suicidegate' press conference. It has not yet become clear whether the shooting has any relation to that case, the bizarrely linked suicides of businessman Sir Jeffrey Patterson, transport minister Beth Davenport, TV producer Jennifer Wilson and teenager James Phillimore. ●

I was NOT suffering from shock!

I knew I should have refused the blanket.

THE ADVENTURE OF THE SECOND STAB

'There was never any question of adding material to the pilot,' says Steven Moffat. 'It was always going to be something that we were going to do from scratch. It would have been terrible. It wouldn't have been good enough.'

And besides, what's the point in a second chance if you don't make some changes?

While, on the surface, the two versions of *A Study in Pink* appear very similar, a great deal has changed in the version that finally saw broadcast. The crew took the opportunity to make some small improvements in the background details. The police women at the Lauriston Gardens murder scene, for example, were wearing skirts in the pilot, which is inaccurate. In the same scene, the earlier recording had been unable to help the fact that it had been lashing down with rain during the outside filming, which was awkward as Sherlock would later go on to say that only Cardiff had experienced that sort of inclement weather in the last few hours. Thankfully this time it was dry.

The house itself was altered, having found a property in Newport that was far more evocative. Despite the constant drive to make everything feel modern there was a real desire to make the inside of the Lauriston Gardens house feel like another, more Gothic world. 'When John meets Sherlock,' says Steven, 'his world changes, he drops down the rabbit hole into somewhere else entirely.'

Actor Jonathan Aris also found himself being shaved for his role as Anderson, the put-upon Medical Examiner, allegedly because a number of people who had seen the pilot assumed he must be a villain. After all, we all know you can't trust a man with facial hair…

A new *Study in Pink* and a new Lauriston Gardens…

Sherlock's 'arch enemy' gets a chance to stage a dramatic first meeting with John Watson...

Aside from these small details, the main change is one of narrative space. With an hour and a half to tell the story, more space could be given to introducing the characters – equally important in a pilot.

'You need to spend time with these people,' says Steven. 'You want to understand them, want to get to know them. You can do that with an hour and a half, you can let yourself have long conversations in Baker Street without pushing aside the mystery.'

We also meet Mycroft, intentionally being led to believe that he is the villainous Moriarty rather than Sherlock's brother. 'Calling him Sherlock's "arch enemy" helped!' says Mark Gatiss.

In the pilot episode, the sandwich shop that sits beneath Sherlock and John's flat was owned by Mrs Hudson, a fact made clear by the awning. Now she has foregone a life in catering to concentrate on being a landlady. Steven and Mark decided that the insurance payout received when her husband went to the electric chair was enough to supplement her rents and keep her for the foreseeable future.

In the pilot, the audience have no idea who shoots Jeff (though, like Sherlock, we may be able to deduce it). As Sherlock is explaining to Lestrade the personality of the gunman he looks up and sees John in the crowd and we realise at the same time that it was him all along. But giving away the secret strengthened

the scene: not only could the camera cut away to John at vital moments, but it also brought him back into the action at a crucial stage.

In many ways, however, the major difference between the pilot and the broadcast version is simply the feel of the piece. The pilot was superbly directed by Coky Giedroyc, the BAFTA nominated director of *The Virgin Queen*, a 2005 BBC miniseries about Elizabeth I, as well as movies such as *Women Talking Dirty*. The broadcast episode was directed by Paul McGuigan, a director who came to the world's attention with his first movie, *The Acid House*, based on the short story collection by author Irvine Welsh. From there he went on to direct *Gangster No. 1* and *Lucky Number Slevin*, a crime picture featuring such Hollywood big-hitters as Bruce Willis, Morgan Freeman and Ben Kingsley. The two versions feel very different and, while Giedroyc's work was assured and deft, McGuigan's style would go on to inform the look of the entire show, most obviously in the much-lauded visual representation of text onscreen.

'The credit for that has to go to Paul McGuigan,' agrees Steven. 'That's something he brought to it and continued to develop. I mean, we all joined in. He directed [episode

Watson's heroic rescue of Sherlock revealed!

three] *The Great Game* first while I was still writing *A Study in Pink* and so I could see where he was going with that.'

'It all started with not wanting to do a voiceover or montage,' adds Mark, 'but still wanting to show Sherlock's thought processes.' Or an approximation of them at least. 'Yes! We don't want to give the game away. We see all the information but we don't see where he's going with it.'

Paul's background in movies also shows as he gives us so much to look at. *Sherlock* is a show that's constantly attractive to the eye; there's very little functional, prosaic storytelling, everything is delivered beautifully to the screen and the audience gets a real sense of this being a lavish and important piece of television.

The show was extremely well received, with Tom Sutcliffe in *The Independent* summing up many people's thoughts when he called it 'a triumph, witty and knowing, without ever undercutting the flair and dazzle of the original'.

Add to that an audience figure of a whopping 9.23 million, and things were off to an amazing start. ∎

A new director's visualisation of Sherlock's world...

A STUDY
IN PINK
BY THE BOOK

A TANGLED SKEIN *A Study in Scarlet* was the very first Sherlock Holmes story, published within the pages of *Beeton's Christmas Annual* in 1887. Like the TV episode it inspired, it concerns a murderous cab driver (Jefferson Hope in the novel, simply 'Jeff' onscreen), though the reader's sympathies probably lie more with Hope than with his victims. The method of murder is the same, a pair of pills, one poisoned one not, as is the fact that the murderer is suffering from an aneurysm.

Thankfully, Steven Moffat's version doesn't have a whopping great Western flashback about Evil Mormons. (Doyle is alleged to have apologised for his unflattering portrayal of the faith, though as the alleging is done by Levi Edgar Young, a descendant of the movement's founder and an authority

on Mormonism, it is perhaps best taken with a pinch of salt.) Steven also sidesteps an awkward moment when the detective decides to test the poison on a terrier that Mrs Hudson conveniently has knocking on death's door: 'Would you mind going down and fetching that poor little devil of a terrier which has been bad so long, and which the landlady wanted you to put out of its misery yesterday?'

THE DISAPPEARANCE OF MR JAMES PHILLIMORE
Sir Arthur Conan Doyle littered his stories with references to other, never seen, cases. Tiny details were given, intended to intrigue the reader. How we long to know the details of the Giant Rat of Sumatra and the matter of the politician, the lighthouse and the trained cormorant. Not to mention what it was that led Isadora Persano, the well-known journalist and duellist, to be found stark staring mad with a matchbox in front of him containing a worm said to be unknown to science. Indeed, many of these unreported cases have gone on to become as famous as the actual stories, becoming the foundation for pastiches by other authors and referenced in other works. Agatha Christie's Hercule Poirot, when illustrating the importance of details to his 'Watson', Captain Hastings, references the dreadful business of the Abernetty family, first brought to Holmes's attention by 'the depth which the parsley had sunk into the butter upon a hot day'.

The disappearance of James Phillimore is one of those cases, mentioned in *The Problem of Thor Bridge* (also referenced when his body is found in the similar-sounding Norbridge sports centre). In the original story, he forms part of a list of unsolved cases: 'A problem without a solution may interest the student, but can hardly fail to annoy the casual reader. Among these unfinished tales is that of Mr James Phillimore, who, stepping back into his own house to get his umbrella, was never more seen in this world.'

THE CRITERION COFFEE BAR

In the original novel, Watson bumps into his old friend Stamford while in the Criterion Bar. The Criterion restaurant and bar adjoin the Criterion Theatre in London's Piccadilly Circus, and it is the setting for John and Stamford's catch-up in the pilot episode. For the broadcast version, it wasn't possible to remount the location filming in the Criterion, so John and Stamford's chat now happens over takeaway coffees, the cups stamped with 'CRITERION'. Sue Vertue, Steven Moffat and Mark Gatiss went for a meal in the Criterion to celebrate the BBC commissioning the show.

A PASSION FOR DEFINITE AND EXACT KNOWLEDGE
In *A Study in Scarlet*, Stamford criticises Holmes for being 'too scientific for my tastes'. He warns Watson of the man's 'passion for definite and exact knowledge' by mentioning that he once witnessed him beating the corpses in the dissection rooms with a stick in order to 'verify how far bruises may be produced after death'. This wonderfully grotesque initial image of our 'hero' has previously been avoided by film-makers, no doubt wary of repelling their audience. Steven and Mark know we're made

of sterner stuff and finally give our jaws the opportunity to drop at the sight of our lead character whipping seven bells out of a stiff.

THE SHIFTING WOUND Doyle was somewhat notorious for his inconsistencies. In the course of four novels and 56 short stories, Mrs Hudson becomes Mrs Turner, John Watson becomes James Watson, and his wife dies only to reappear and then vanish again. Fans of the original stories have, of course, wound themselves in pleasurable knots attempting to explain these contradictions. In truth, they happened simply because Doyle slipped up. One of these discrepancies concerns the wound that saw Watson pensioned out of the army. In *A Study in Scarlet*, it's in his shoulder (grazing the subclavian artery, in fact); in *A Sign of Four*, it's in his leg. Later, in *The Noble Bachelor*, Doyle gives up trying to remember and settles for it being in 'one of his limbs'. The solution for this in *Sherlock*, of course, is that John appears to be wounded in both locations – and the limp turns out to be psychosomatic.

Sherlock's question of whether John had been in 'Afghanistan or Iraq?' is also a direct link back to the original novel, though in *A Study in Scarlet* the detective was unequivocal in his deduction that it had been Afghanistan. In fairness this owes more to the political situation of the time and the conclusion of the Second Anglo-Afghan War than any uncertainty on the modern-day Sherlock's part.

A BROWN STUDY When discussing the possibility of sharing rooms, both the modern and original Sherlock Holmes suggest it would be sensible for them to know the worst of each other. His habits of playing the violin and not talking for days on end remain utterly unchanged, though his tobacco consumption has been ejected, along with Watson's bull-terrier.

I'M YOUR LANDLADY, NOT YOUR HOUSEKEEPER Of course, in the original stories Mrs Hudson certainly was their housekeeper, but housekeepers are thin on the ground these days.

LETTER KNIFE Holmes has always chosen to keep certain correspondence affixed to his mantelpiece with a knife, bills and divorce cases, presumably.

FROM CLARA x Sherlock's analysis of John's mobile phone mirrors Holmes's examination of Watson's pocket watch in *The Sign of Four*. Despite the difference in objects, the analysis is extremely similar; scratches from where a key has been inserted to wind the watch up point to Watson's brother being a drunk ('you'll seldom find a drunk's without them'), with scratches around his phone's charge port leading to the same deduction from Sherlock. It is worth noting that Doyle's father was an alcoholic and so he was writing from some experience.

THE GAME IS ON! Catchphrases are misleading things: nine times out of ten they were probably not uttered in the original source material. Not that this makes them any less entrenched in the cultural baggage of a character of course – whether Captain James Tiberius Kirk ever shouted 'Beam me up, Scotty!' or not, most people think he did. Sherlock Holmes's most famous utterance (and gift to bad joke writers everywhere) is, of course, 'Elementary, my dear Watson!' It's a phrase that was never uttered in any of the Doyle novels or stories, yet it is as much a part of the character now as the deerstalker and the calabash pipe (and let's not get into the legitimacy of those either, or we shall be here all day). Second place in the league table of Things People Expect Sherlock Holmes To Cry With Dramatic Abandon goes to 'Come, Watson, the game is afoot!' or variations thereon. This did appear in Doyle. In *The Adventure of the Abbey Grange*, it was shouted at a poor sleeping Watson at the crack of dawn. Sleep didn't always come easily (or last long) when you shared rooms with the world's foremost consulting detective. Of course, using the word 'afoot' in this day and age would mark you out as being as strange and archaic as a horse-drawn gas-lamp, so Steven Moffat has sensibly substituted the word 'on'.

If inconvenient,
come anyway.
SH

COME ANYWAY

Sherlock sends John a text message asking him to meet him at Baker Street 'if convenient'. This is followed seconds later by a text message saying 'If inconvenient, come anyway.' This is a direct reference to a telegram sent at the opening of *The Adventure of the Creeping Man*: 'Come at once if convenient – if inconvenient, come all the same. S. H.' Holmes wishes to discuss his latest case (Watson describes himself as a 'whetstone' to Holmes's mind, his presence helps bring clarity, even if only when used as a sounding board), whereas onscreen Holmes merely wishes to borrow John's mobile phone.

RACHE

In the original novel, Doyle has Lestrade jump to the obvious conclusion that the murder victim (the wonderfully named Enoch Drebber) was trying to write 'Rachel' but was unable to finish. Holmes scoffs at this and suggests that the word is in fact complete: 'Rache', German for 'revenge'. In the episode, this is reversed with the German-literate Anderson suggesting 'Rache' while Sherlock plumps for 'Rachel'.

A THREE-PATCH PROBLEM

The original Holmes often seemed to subsist entirely on tobacco fumes, often forgoing food for tobacco. He would store his rough Turkish blend in a Persian slipper hanging from the fireplace. When faced with a particularly knotty problem, Holmes would announce it a 'three-pipe problem', defining the amount of tobacco and time it would take for him to come to his conclusion. These days it's 'impossible to sustain a smoking habit in London', so Sherlock has ditched the fags in favour of nicotine patches. The fact that he can wear three at a time certainly shows that he is a man who has developed an impressive tolerance to nicotine, the effects of overdosing on which can be fatal.

But then Sherlock is clearly a man with something of a pharmaceutical background, as is hinted by his somewhat uncomfortable response to Lestrade's men searching the flat. Doyle's Holmes, of course, would occasionally inject a seven per cent solution of cocaine, self-medicating against the crippling boredom that struck him whenever without a case. ■

THE ADVENTURE OF THE DYSFUNCTIONAL DETECTIVE

So who is Sherlock Holmes? The cleverest person in the room. Self-proclaimed 'high-functioning sociopath'. Addict – of mental stimulation above all else. He is the thinker; the logician; the detective; the magician, achieving the seemingly impossible through skill and misdirection.

'He has one whopping advantage over magicians, though,' says Steven Moffat. 'This is where Doyle is right and magicians are wrong: always tell them how the trick is done! I saw a magic act in Edinburgh where you went to see the magic act, a very good magic act, and then you went back an hour later and he showed you how every single trick was done. And I have to say that knowing did not spoil it. Sherlock Holmes tells you how the trick is done. However much you may hate him, you want to listen to the next thing he says. You'd *really* hate him if he said, "I'm going to do all this and then not tell you how!"'

And plenty of people *do* hate him. After all, he makes very little attempt to be likeable.

'People get a vicarious thrill out of that,' admits Benedict Cumberbatch, 'because Holmes doesn't suffer mediocrity. He's somebody who is constantly frustrated by the mediocre or everyday. But the audience like him because they don't have to live with him, they can just sit back and enjoy him. He's blissfully rude, entertainingly irreverent, bordering on sociopathic. People get a real thrill out of that.'

Certainly Sherlock must be hard to live with. Mind you, as anyone who has ever shared a flat will know, there are far worse habits to be found in one's flatmate than playing the violin and not talking for days on end.

'We had discussions right at the beginning with the BBC,' says Mark Gatiss, 'about whether it was possible to have an unlikeable hero at the heart of your show. Of course *House*

Sherlock Holmes: not the easiest person to like

proved that was fine; he's horrid but everyone adores him!'

Indeed, *House* owes a great debt to Holmes, as acknowledged in the intentional pun of the title as well as the initials of his one true friend Dr James Wilson. Hugh Laurie's Gregory House does have more of a sex life – just – but this hasn't stopped Benedict Cumberbatch becoming something of a sex symbol, despite the fact that his character sees love as nothing more than a chemical imbalance. 'I was stopped on the street,' he says, 'and thanked on behalf of asexuals everywhere.'

There are worse habits a flatmate can have than playing the violin

Benedict has since been voted Sexiest Man in the World by readers of *The Sun*. Obviously Sherlock is managing to charm some people.

'I think he can be charming,' says Benedict. 'It's something he turns on in order to get something! But what's really interesting and powerful about him is his ability to see adventure in the smallest of detail. Everything is a potential spark for adventure, and that's a very thrilling thing.'

'We like our heroes to be complex,' he continues. 'We don't like two-dimensional stereotypes. They don't last very long. Also, for an actor, it's a lot more fun to play someone who has shape and edge than someone who has been softened and "vanillafied".'

Playing such characters can take its toll, of course. Jeremy Brett was warned not to take the part in the 1980s. Robert Stephens warned him

that it was a role that would send him mad. Was he right?

'With the greatest respect,' says Benedict, 'Brett was a very troubled man, and I think that advice was probably personally tailored. There's nothing about Holmes that's a problem if you're an actor that has anything else to do in their life. As long as he isn't *all-consuming*. I've played people who are far madder. I don't believe there's a mystical connection between a character and a performer. You can treat these things with too much care and the business of acting becomes bound in prurient superstition.

'You get caught up in fear and worry and anxiety and then you can't play it. That's why I think Brett's interpretation, masterful though it is, is always going to be something of its own. It becomes something that isn't Sherlock Holmes.' He laughs. 'Still, I'm 36. I've got plenty of time to lose it yet...'

Hugh Laurie's House

Jeremy Brett's Holmes

CASE NOTES:

The Blind Banker

Oh. The one where a clearly stupid woman mistakes you for me.

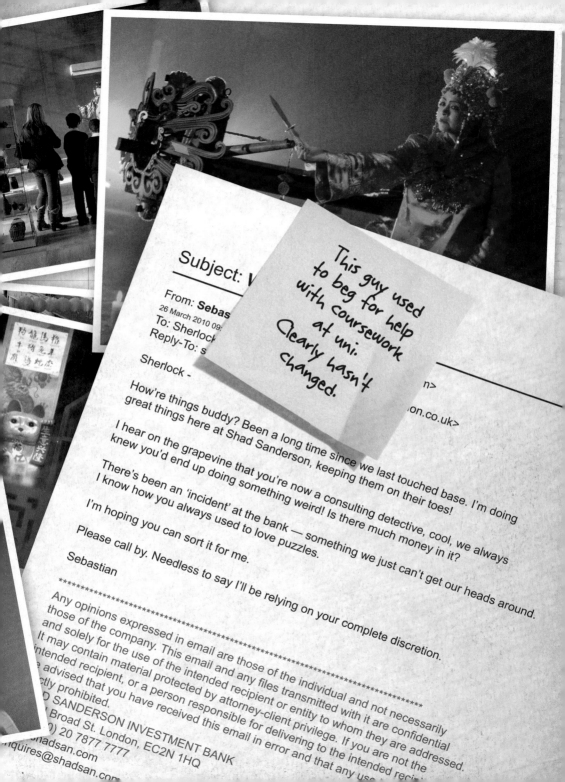

Subject: W...

From: Sebas...
26 March 2010 09:...
To: Sherlock...
Reply-To: s...

Sherlock -

How're things buddy? Been a long time since we last touched base. I'm doing great things here at Shad Sanderson, keeping them on their toes!

I hear on the grapevine that you're now a consulting detective, cool, we always knew you'd end up doing something weird! Is there much money in it?

There's been an 'incident' at the bank — something we just can't get our heads around. I know how you always used to love puzzles.

I'm hoping you can sort it for me.

Please call by. Needless to say I'll be relying on your complete discretion.

Sebastian

****
Any opinions expressed in email are those of the individual and not necessarily those of the company. This email and any files transmitted with it are confidential and solely for the use of the intended recipient or entity to whom they are addressed. It may contain material protected by attorney-client privilege. If you are not the intended recipient, or a person responsible for delivering to the intended recipient, be advised that you have received this email in error and that any use... ...ctly prohibited.
...D SANDERSON INVESTMENT BANK
... Broad St. London, EC2N 1HQ
...0) 20 7877 7777
...shadsan.com
...quires@shadsan.com

Handwritten note: This guy used to beg for help with coursework at uni. Clearly hasn't changed.

The Blind Banker

Sir William Shad, former chairman. Office broken into and defaced within a one-minute window in the security camera footage.

All rooms (from offices to storage cupboards) are controlled from a central-locking protocol within the security software. According to the software the door was never opened.

Defaced portrait of Sir William. Some kind of threat? An attack against the banking system?

So speaks the only man alive to lose in a fight with a chip and pin machine.

On the wall next to the portrait. Some form of code?

EDW

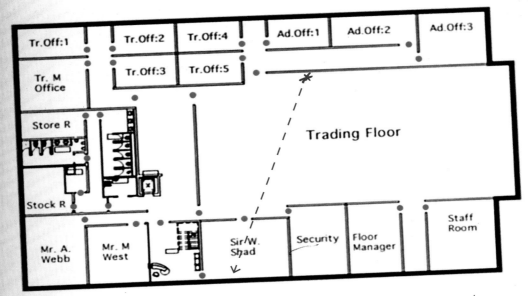

* Optimum line of sight for the graffiti in Shad's office. Edward Van Coon, the head of the Hong Kong desk. The message was aimed at him.

When you've finished with your Girl's Scrapbook, could you come and find me? I have something Extremely Obvious that needs stating.

Certainly. How about:
'Most people think I'm mad to put up with you.'

Me included.

The Blind Banker

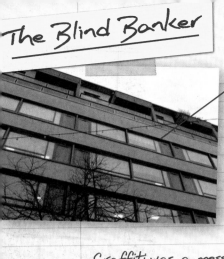

105 Albert Dock, 17a New Wharf Road.

Sebastian Wilkes had known Van Coon from Oxford. As Van Coon had spent a lot of time in Asia, Wilkes gave him the Hong Kong accounts.

Van Coon found dead in his flat. Gun in hand. Bullet wound to the right temple. The initial assumption was that he had taken his own life.

Graffiti was a message, but why not simply contact Van Coon direct? The message must be a threat, a demand given to someone who had ignored other attempts at communication.

Initial assumption by the police and passing GPs.

Some of us remember that it's a mistake to theorise without all the facts.

- Coffee table to left of the chair
- coffee mug on table has handle pointing to the left
- left-hand power sockets habitually used
- pen and paper to the left of the phone
- butter knife in the kitchen with butter on the right-hand side of the blade.

CONCLUSION: EDDIE VAN COON WAS LEFT-HANDED.

Left-handed people do not shoot themselves on the right side of their head.

Judging by the dirty clothes in his still-unpacked case, Van Coon had been away for three days.

Sherlock is adamant that Van Coon was shot by someone else, the bullet in his head will not match his gun. Van Coon likely fired in retaliation but the bullet went out of the open window.

Sadly the police are determined to follow the easier route of assuming it's a suicide. DI Dimmock, another 'Scotland Yarder' to ~~suffer~~ enjoy Sherlock's ~~temper~~ mental improvements

Journalist Slain In Impossible Murder

LAST NIGHT, Brian Lukis, 41, a freelance journalist from Earl's Court, was murdered by an assailant who appears capable of walking through walls. Police are baffled. The investigation has turned up no clue as to how the murderer gained access to Lukis' flat, all doors and windows were locked from the inside and there was no sign of a break-in. The investigation continues.

Lukis murdered in similar circumstances to Van Coon. 'They think they're safe,' Sherlock says, 'because they live high off the ground. But we're dealing with a murderer who can climb.'

Did I say that? I'm getting as overly dramatic as you.

Book stamped with the date of Lukis' death led us to the shelves of West Kensington Library.

NOV 05 2009
DEC 18 2009
MAR 24 2010

The Blind Banker

The same graffiti
again - Lukis received
an identical threat
before his death.

According to 'Raz'
(Sherlock's 'expert' on
graffiti) the paint 'is
like Michigan, hardcore
propellant, I'd say
zinc'. Whatever that's
supposed to mean.

If you ever use this
many quotation
marks in a sentence
again I'll have the
locks changed while
you're out.

17th March, Van Coon
flew into Dalian Airport
in the Liaoning Province,
Northeast China.

Zhuang Airlines

Boarding Pass

NAME LUKIS/BRIAN

TO   DALIAN DLC

FROM LONDON LHR

ZHUANG AIRLINES

AS 601   U   ZA 0214

A21 950P

ELECTRONIC
43W   **24E**

Lukis had also visited Dalian at around the same time. What was the purpose of their trip? Did they meet?

We tracked Van Coon's movements on his return.

Van Coon had lunch.

Van Coon had taken something heavy into town (in a taxi) delivered it and then gone straight to his office. Lukis had written down the address of a shop on Shaftesbury Avenue.

PIAZZA   ESPRESSO BAR

PIAZZA
ESPRESSO BAR
ITALIANO
TELEPHONE #: 020 7946 0864

EFT NBR, 008654170421006

POS : 188653064101110

MAESTRO

cenced Taxi Receipt
Date 22/3/10.
Time 10:35.
Amount £ 18.50

57

Thank you for your custom

Signed ....

● London Underground   ● London Underground

22MAR10   DAY SINGLE   4.80

22 MCH 10   PICCADILLY

>> << . . .   >> << . . . >> << . . .   >> << .

001134   29   0500   22MCH10   13.30   235322

This side up • Not for resale
Issued subject to conditions - see over

This side up • Not for resale
Issued subject to conditions - see over

The Lucky Cat Emporium
93 Shaftesbury Avenue
Soho W1D

The Blind Banker

Symbols are Hang Zhou, an ancient Chinese number system.

Straight line translate as '1', the other graffiti translates as '5' so the message was '15'.

The singular of 'graffiti' is 'graffito'! Winning these little battles will be your first step towards creating readable prose on your blog.

Both men recently in China and visited Lucky Cat Emporium immediately on their return. What were they bringing into the country?

And which one got light-fingered?
Both were threatened so their masters didn't know either. Easy solution: kill them both.

Never work in H.R.

Is that something to do with the Queen? How could you work inside the Queen and retain your head?

Soo Lin Yao, lived above the shop.
Judging by a rain-soaked Yellow Pages
outside her door she hadn't been home
for a few days. Could she be the contact
rather than the owners of the shop?

After sneaking in via the fire escape
(and leaving me stood outside like an idiot),
Sherlock deduced that someone else had
also broken in recently by their signs of
entry, and the size 8 shoe-print on the rug.

We had found our
acrobatic assassin.
And another clue...

**Only one
way to
find out...**

**And the
strangulation
marks around
my throat.**

NATIONAL
ANTIQUITIES
MUSEUM

Soo Lin

Please ring me

Tell me you're

OK

Andy

The Blind Banker

Soo Lin had also received a message:

NATIONAL
ANTIQUITIES
MUS...

And she was now nowhere
to be found.

All we could do was follow the
graffiti, scouring the streets
for more to work from.

From the South Bank...

... to London Bridge.

Finally, I came across this:

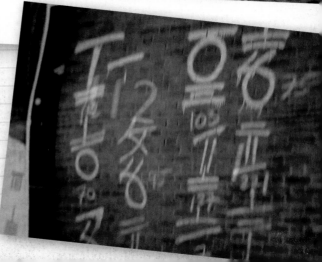

Sherlock could translate the Hang Zhou into numbers.

But what did the numbers mean? We needed someone who understood the code.

The Blind Banker

Returning to the museum, Sherlock
noticed that the teapots that Soo
Lin cared for had continued to be
maintained. Perhaps she hadn't run
as far away as we might have thought?

We found Soo Lin still at the museum
where she had been hiding all that
time. At first she was frightened
but somehow Sherlock managed to
convince her he was friendly.

It's called charm,
I don't use it on
you because you're
mad enough to
put up with me
without it.

She showed us a tattoo on the sole of her foot.

Sherlock identified it as the mark of a Tong, a Chinese secret
society or gang. This was the Tong of the Black Lotus and Soo
Lin had worked for them, smuggling drugs into Hong Kong, for
most of her life. Now she had tried to escape but they had
found her and insisted she continue to work for them.

But having tried to hide, her life was now in danger, the Tong's
enforcer on her trail. Zhi Zhu, 'The Spider', the acrobatic
assassin who had already killed Van Coon and Lukis, was Soo
Lin's brother.

We had failed, Soo Lin was dead at the hand of her brother,
under orders from General Shan, head of the Tong of the
Black Lotus.

POLICE REP

OFFICER: Sgt. Philip Jarrett

DATE: 25th March 2010

I was called to the National Antiquities Museum after a pair of Dutch tourists had reported hearing gunshots fired from inside the building. It was thirteen minutes past one in the morning when I arrived and I found the front doors unlocked. Deciding that the call was genuine, I called for backup and began looking for the local security.

The security was limited to one terrified Welshman who I found hiding behind what a sign informed me to be a 16th-century burial casket. Having managed to avoid being brained by the security guard's torch, I was waiting for backup as per regulations when a gentleman appeared through the doors that led to the Egyptian Room. He was armed with what I later discovered to be a fossilised human leg bone and it was only through my quick intervention that he didn't beat the security guard senseless with it. I was later informed that the man was Sherlock Holmes and that he was known to the Met having previously assisted us in a freelance capacity. At the time I was more inclined to consider him the enemy, though he was quick to restrain himself once he realised I was a police officer.

Mr Holmes explained that he and his colleague, Dr John Watson (also known to the department) had been pursuing an investigation, interviewing one of the staff, when they became aware that someone else was in the building and that their interviewee might be in some danger. Quite what they were doing interviewing her so far after opening hours was never satisfactorily explained. In fact, after a few minutes of questioning, Mr Holmes simply insisted that I 'discuss it with Dim of the Yard' (I later discovered he was referring to DI Dimmock) and returned to the Egyptian Room.

Giving chase I was led eventually to where his colleague was attempting, unsuccessfully, to administer to Miss Soo Lin Yao, employee of the museum and victim of the unnamed gunman who had by all

But we knew what they had been smuggling: valuable Chinese relics.

Sale of a pair of vases, the dates of which matched up with a recent visit to China for both Lukis and Van Coon.

Lot Description

A PAIR OF CHINESE MING VASES CHENGUA *(1447 - 1487)*

Arrived from China 4 days ago.

Two undiscovered treasures from the East.

Double-gourd shaped vase. Painted white porcelain, with blue floral design incorporated.

ESTIMATE: £400,000–£500,000 ($619,006–$773,758)

Sale Information:

Sale 5681

Crispians Auction – Chinese and other Asian Works of Art

Source – Anonymous

March

	Tuesday	Wednesday	Thursday
	2 .00 - Trail Meeting .30 - Conference .30 - Lunch @pin .20 - Training .45 - Meet with D Pring	**3** 09.00 - Interview 10.30 - Call CEO 13.30 - Lunch w Dom 17.30 - Conf call off	**4** 09.00 - Trail Me 10.30 - Confere 13.30 - Lunch w 14.20 - Training 15.45 - Meet w
	9 09.00 - Staff meeting 10.30 - Conference 13.30 - Lunch @pin 15.45 - Meet with D Pring	**10** 09.00 - Call Tim 10.30 - Annual Rev 13.30 - Lunch @pin 14.20 - Meeting	**11** 09.00 - T Mor 10.30 - Confe 13.30 - Lunch 14.20 - Train 15.45 - Meet
	16 09.00 - G Anderson 10.30 - Conference 13.30 - Lunch w Matt 14.20 - Training	**17** Dalian	**18** Dalian
	23 09.00 - Mid briefing 10.30 - S Peel 13.30 - Lunch @pin 14.20 - Training 15.45 - Conf call p/p	**24** 09.00 - Meeting 13.30 - Lunch @pin 14.20 - Training 15.45 - Meet with D Pring	**25** 09.00 - Tr 10.30 - Cd 13.30 - Lu 14.20 - T 15.45 - M
	30 09.30 - Staff Meeting 10.30 - Conference 13.30 - Lunch @pin 14.20 - Interview	**31** 10.30 - Conference 13.30 - Lunch w Jess 14.20 - H Parsons 15.45 - Meet with D Pring	

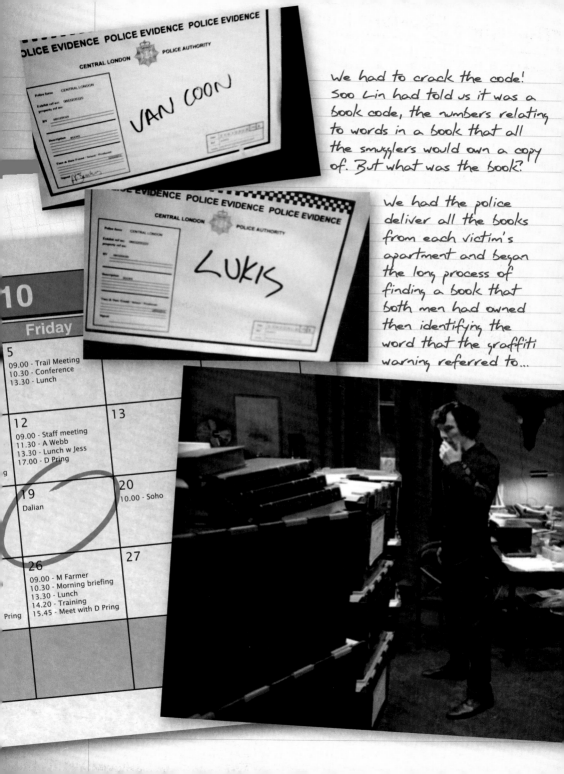

POLICE EVIDENCE POLICE EVIDENCE POLICE EVIDENCE

CENTRAL LONDON POLICE AUTHORITY

VAN COON

POLICE EVIDENCE POLICE EVIDENCE POLICE EVIDENCE

CENTRAL LONDON POLICE AUTHORITY

LUKIS

We had to crack the code! Soo Lin had told us it was a book code, the numbers relating to words in a book that all the smugglers would own a copy of. But what was the book?

We had the police deliver all the books from each victim's apartment and began the long process of finding a book that both men had owned then identifying the word that the graffiti warning referred to...

10

Friday

5
09.00 - Trail Meeting
10.30 - Conference
13.30 - Lunch

12
09.00 - Staff meeting
11.30 - A Webb
13.30 - Lunch w Jess
17.00 - D Pring

13

19
Dalian

20
10.00 - Soho

26
09.00 - M Farmer
10.30 - Morning briefing
13.30 - Lunch
14.20 - Training
15.45 - Meet with D Pring

27

Pring

The Blind Banker

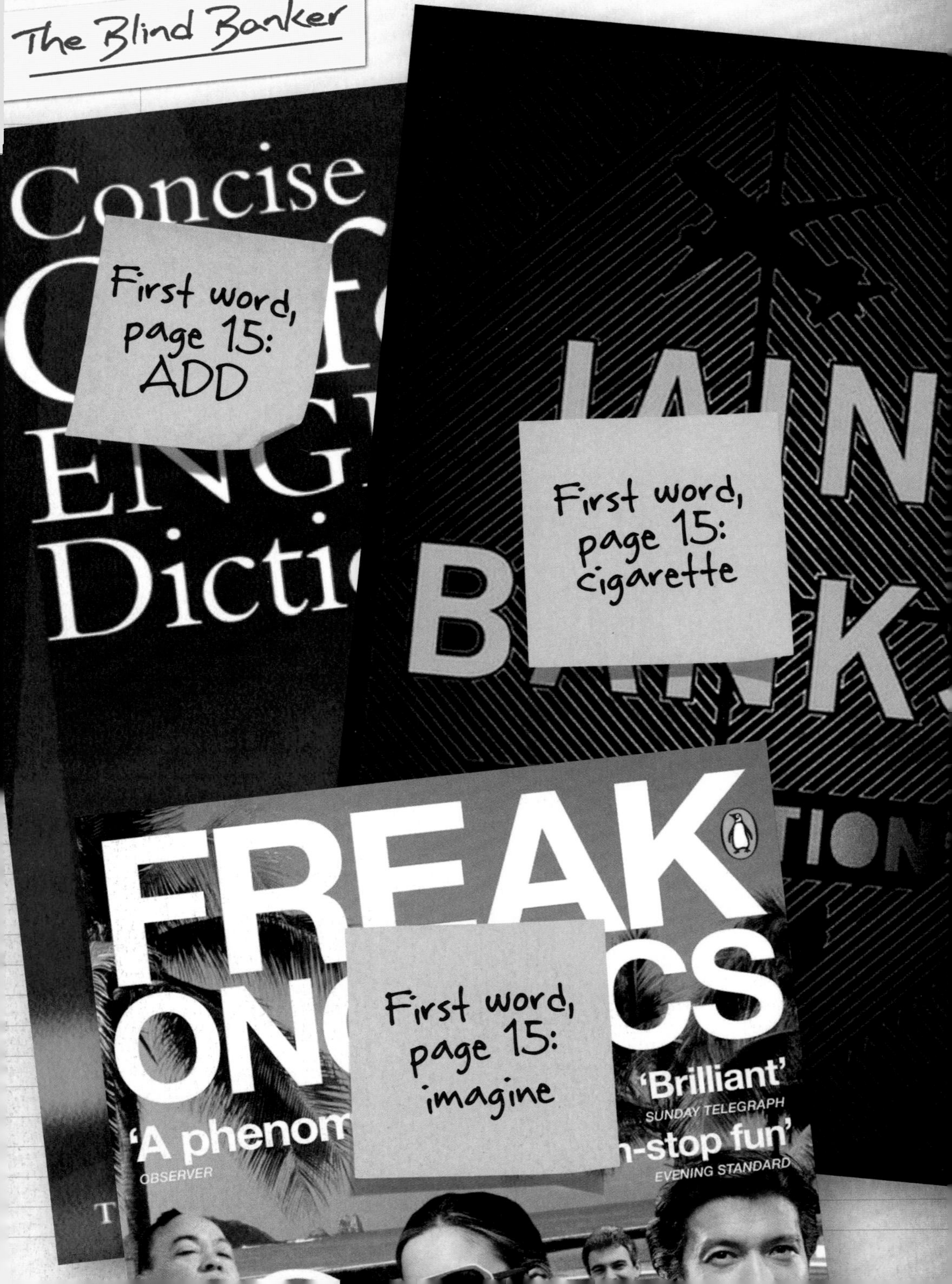
Concise
ENG
Dicti
First word, page 15: ADD
IAIN
B
K
First word, page 15: cigarette
TION
FREAK
ON
CS
First word, page 15: imagine
'A phenom
OBSERVER
'Brilliant'
SUNDAY TELEGRAPH
n-stop fun'
EVENING STANDARD

We worked through the night but felt we were no closer by dawn.

Having finally found some work I'd also found a date, Sarah Sawyer who worked at the same practice. When Sherlock suggested I took her to the circus for an unusual night out I almost thought he was being considerate. Almost. One fight with deadly Tong assassins undercover as circus performers later...

Best. Date. Ever.
Stop complaining.

Which one was Sarah?
The one with all
the teeth or all
the freckles?

Neither.
I think.

£12.00   SECTION: FLOOR   ADMISSION

QUIC   26/03/10   QUICKTICKET PRESENT   GENERAL ADMIS

£12   08:00PM   YELLOW DRAGON

26   GA   NEW

08   RING:

5/0   1305486-30   DEADLY CHINESE   the
08:0   GA   BIRD-SPIDER   MONKEY KING

GA   1305486-23

1305486-22   NT & SKILLED PERFORMERS WILL THRILL YOU WITH ANCIENT SKILLS,
PRACTICED IN CHINA FOR OVER A THOUSAND YEARS

YELLOW DRAGON
CIRCUS
Box Office
Tel: 020 79460470

The Blind Banker

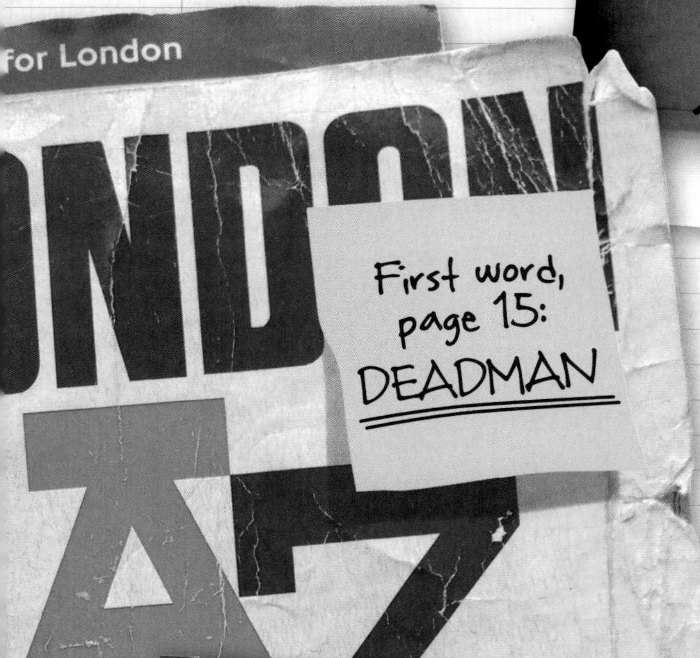

for London

LONDON A-Z

15   1

First word,
page 15:
DEADMAN

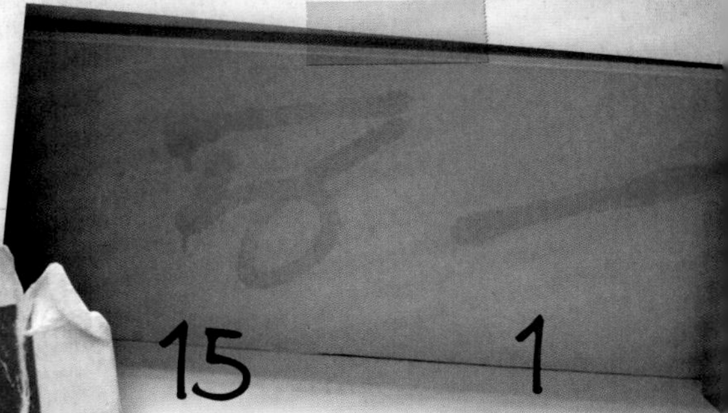

The London A-Z!
A book that they all
owned, and the entry
relating to the coded
message left at the bank
and the library, the first
word on the fifteenth
page: DEADMAN. A
death threat, one that
was delivered soon after
they had received it. We
had the code cracked!

nine

mill

for

jade

pin

dragon

den

black

tramway

A jade pin valued at nine million pounds, no wonder Van Coon gave in to temptation!

Found the Tong, found the pin, case closed!

There was the small matter of my and Sarah's kidnapping and near death!

Small matter. Yes. Just that. I saved you didn't I? Crossbows and excitement.

Second. Best. Date. Ever.

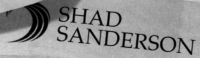
SHAD SANDERSON

PAY MR S HOLMES

£10,000,000s	£1,000,000s	£100,000s	£10,000s	£1,000s	£100s	£10s	UNITS
ZERO	ZERO	ZERO	ZERO	FIVE	ZERO	ZERO	ZERO

AMO___ __ POUNDS IN WORDS

PENCE ___

DATE 29/03/10

£ 5,000.00

FOR AND ON BEHALF OF
SHAD SANDERSON

Yes! Idiot! She shot herself in the forehead with a sniper rifle!

How is this man able to get dressed in the morning let alone function as a police officer?

POLICE

OFFICER: DI Dimmock

CASE SUMMARY

Having always been suspicious of the deaths of Mr Eddie Van Coon and Adrian Lukis I had continued to investigate the matter alongside the rest of my casework. Correctly concluding that they had both been murdered by a Chinese criminal organisation known as the Tong of the Black Lotus, I traced the Tong to the Yellow Dragon Circus, a performance troupe they used as cover for their operations. Unfortunately I narrowly missed capturing the gang on that occasion.

Later that night, we cornered the majority of the gang during an operation staged at the disused Holborn Tramway statio___ group's leader, General Shan, escaped ___ ___ ___ She had shot herself ___

THE ADVENTURE OF THE LOYAL DOCTOR

'Conan Doyle plays fast and loose with Watson,' admits Steven Moffat. 'He was always emphatic that Watson was not a fool, and yet there are many stories that hinge on the fact that he's completely stupid! You cannot read the start of *The Dancing Men* without thinking Watson's a bit of an idiot. Holmes tells him, "You'll say all this is absurdly simple in a few minutes," and he does!'

'It wouldn't work if Watson was a complete fool,' Mark Gatiss points out, 'because you'd lose respect for Sherlock Holmes. Besides if he can't tie his own shoelaces, then how did he ever become a doctor?'

'He's definitely not a genius,' continues Steven. 'By Sherlock Holmes's standards he's a complete moron because *everybody* is, but what he is to Sherlock Holmes is the first man he'd trust. To be a man that an incredibly perceptive genius chooses to trust, you must be pretty exceptional. Not in the ways that Sherlock Holmes is exceptional, but Sherlock Holmes doesn't need another brain. John Watson is the most reliable, competent man that Sherlock knows.'

No, Sherlock doesn't need another brain. But he could benefit from an extra heart.

'People are just a part of the puzzle to Sherlock,' says Martin Freeman, 'but Watson invests emotion in them. He cares. It's a very good balance to have as a double act. They're constantly righting themselves so that you get one human being in the end.'

'Sherlock's just ice,' agrees Benedict Cumberbatch. 'Watson completes him.'

It took John a while to realise he was holding the map upside down

John and Sherlock: the perfect double act

Something Watson shares with Martin Freeman, perhaps – Benedict, during auditions, told the producers that Martin 'makes my game better'.

Some of Watson's skills also run the risk of being overshadowed in the light of his more spectacular flatmate. He is an accomplished doctor, a decent shot, played clarinet at school and possesses an ASBO (for defacing public property). He also loves danger.

'He misses the theatre of war,' says Steven, 'the thrill of that, the pumping adrenalin, the constant danger. He sees in Holmes a chance to feel all that again, to find a new war to fight.'

Finally, Watson is also the catalyst for change. He is the critical audience to Sherlock, the man who can judge his deficiencies as well as his strengths. The man who can finally teach him right or wrong.

'He's the moral barometer,' says Martin. 'Sherlock doesn't always consider the rights and wrongs of what he does. That's what Watson's for because he's simply a decent, ordinary man.' ∎

CASE NOTES:

The Great Game

The one where I was REALLY clever.

As opposed to just moderately clever, yes.

Town

Don't miss out on the best entertainment in town!

Your complete guide to the BIG films this year!

Win tickets to a big show ng this

HICKMAN GALLERY

THE LOST VERME

Not how I like to start the day. Having spent the night at Sarah's I woke to news that there had been an explosion on Baker Street.

Explosion rocks Marylebone

THIS MORNING emergency services rushed to an explosion on Baker Street, just round the corner from Madame Tussaud's in Central London. Despite initial concerns of terrorist involvement, police are now satisfied that the explosion was caused by a gas leak at number 220, a residential address, and was not premeditated.

The Great Game

Thankfully everything - and everyone -
was all right at 221b though Sherlock
continued to be in a poisonous mood,
having no cases to occupy him.

Even a visit from Mycroft didn't cheer
him up. Though he wasn't close with
his brother, you'd have thought the
chance at a new mystery would have
had an effect. No. It was down to
me to take the following notes while
Sherlock just sulked and acted as
if his brother had brought the
smell of drains in with him.

It has always been thus.
You should have seen
him when we were boys:
all I had to do was
walk into the room
and he'd be flinging
his dinner at me.
Mother despaired.
         -M.

Not you too,
Mycroft! Will
everyone please
leave my notes
ALONE.

Notes taken during interview with Mycroft:

* Andrew West, known as 'Westie' to his
friends. Worked for MI6 as a clerk at
Vauxhall Cross. Left his fiancée at 10.30pm,
saying he had to go and see someone.

* Later found dead beside the tracks at
Battersea Station, head bashed in.
Presumably hit by a train.

* M.O.D. been working on a new missile defence
program, the Bruce Partington Program. Plans
for it were on a memory stick that went
missing. West the only suspect for their theft.

* Oyster card unused, no ticket found on the
body, how did he get on the train?

Just a quick
security check.
On the subject
of which ...

know all that would
you? I'd hate to have
the security services
assassinating my
brother's flatmate.
Or should I say
'carer'?

Finally, a summons from Lestrade got Sherlock out of the house. Apparently the 'gas leak' had been nothing of the sort. A planned explosion had destroyed the house leaving only a strongbox containing a small parcel addressed to Sherlock.

Inside there was a phone. A painstaking replica of the one owned by Jennifer Wilson.

When Sherlock opened the phone, it received a text: five 'pips' from the speaking clock and a picture of an empty room.

Sherlock recognised the empty room as being from the flat below us: 221c. In the flat was a pair of trainers.

Five pips, John, as in orange or apple pips, some secret societies used to send them as a warning.

Sherlock Holmes

The Great Game

The mobile rang and Sherlock received a call.

Sherlock's call transcript —

Caller: Hello Sexy.

Me: Who's this?

Caller: I've sent you a little puzzle to say 'Hi'!...
Me: Who's talking?
Why are you crying?

Caller: I'm not crying, I'm typing and this stupid bitch is reading it out... 12 hours to solve my puzzle, Sherlock, or I'm going to be so naughty.

Sherlock decamped to St Bart's to analyse the trainers in detail.

- Limited edition, two blue stripes, 1989.
- Well loved, wiped clean whenever dirty.
- Laces changed four times.
- Skin flakes from fingers rubbing against laces show owner had eczema.
- Worn on one side more than the other, owner had weak arches.
- Traces of Sussex mud covered over with London mud. Owner came from Sussex to London but the much-loved shoes (and presumably their owner) never returned.

Jim Zucco

DYNAMIC ASTEROID

IT & Web Design
07698 164 400
jim@dynamicasteroid.com

The Carl Powers case was where Sherlock started, determined to prove that not all was as it appeared to be. When he heard that the boy's shoes had been missing he knew that foul play had been involved (the shoes could hardly have vanished on their own, someone had taken them). But the police refused to listen.

Nothing changes.

Tragedy at school swimming tournament

TRAGEDY HIT a school swimming tournament being held at the Atwill-Porter Baths in Bounds Green yesterday. Pupils from twelve different schools were competing in the Tony Higgins Cup, a national competition founded twelve years ago and designed to reward excellence in youth sports.

Carl Powers, a pupil from the Daniell Street Comprehensive in Brighton, was a favourite to win in the 1000 metres Freestyle but suffered from an unspecified fit halfway through the race. By the time medical staff had taken him from the water and attempted to assist it was too late. Staff at the Atwill-Porter Baths have insisted that there was no negligence on the part of either themselves or the event organisers though an enquiry will naturally take place.

The hostage was released. A woman named Karen Verne who had been abducted from her Cornwall home by two men wearing masks. She had been forced to drive to a local supermarket car park where she had been wired up with explosives.

SOLVED -
Pair of trainers belonging to Carl Powers (1978-1989)
Botulinum toxin still present. Apply 221b Baker street.

The Great Game

But it wasn't long before
Sherlock received another
text (four pips this time).
And a picture of a car...

BJ06 ZH

CONFIDENTIAL

TRANSCRIPT ON LINE TAP: 07796649870

REQUESTED BY: DI LESTRADE
AUTHORISED BY: CHIEF COMMISSIONER BLAND

CALLER: It's OK that you've gone to the police but don't rely on them.
Clever you, guessing about Carl Powers, I never liked him.
Carl laughed at me so I stopped him laughing. This is about
you and me. The balance of life, Sherlock, but don't worry,
I can soon fix that. You solved my last puzzle in nine hou~
this time you have eight.

Lestrade traced the car as a rental
leased in the name of Ian Monkford. It
had been abandoned just south of the river.

With what looked like a good few pints
of Ian Monkford still inside it.

Monkford's wife admitted her husband
had been depressed for months. He'd
hired the car for a business trip as
he'd forgotten to renew the insurance
on their own car. This was not like
him. Sherlock found all this out by
pretending to be a weeping friend of
Monkford's. Because he's evil.

Oh God! You don't
really think I'm evil,
do you? I just find
it hard to access
my emotions.
With your help
I could change!

You're doing
it again,
aren't you?

Yes.

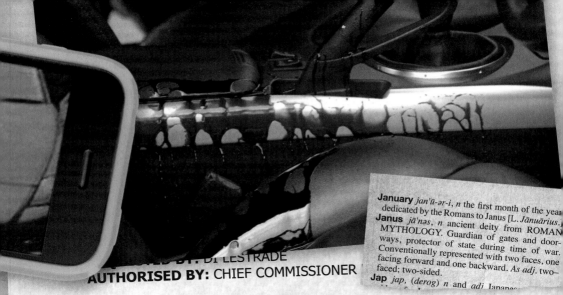

January *jan'ū-ǝr-i*, *n* the first month of the year, dedicated by the Romans to Janus [L. *Jānuārius*.] **Janus** *jā'nas*, *n* ancient deity from ROMAN MYTHOLOGY. Guardian of gates and doorways, protector of state during time of war. Conventionally represented with two faces, one facing forward and one backward. *As adj.* two—faced; two-sided.
Jap *jap*, (*derog*) *n* and *adj* Japanese

~~~~ED BY: DI LESTRADE
AUTHORISED BY: CHIEF COMMISSIONER

CALLER:	The clue's in the name Janus cars.
SHERLOCK HOLMES:	Why would you be giving me a clue?
CALLER:	Why does anyone do anything? Because I'm bored. We were made for each other, Sherlock.
SHERLOCK HOLMES:	Then talk to me in your own voice.
CALLER:	Patience.

Car hire company, Janus Cars, run by Steve Ewart, who Sherlock was only too quick to analyse.

* Conspicuous tan line, claims it's from a sunbed but what sort of idiot would wear a shirt on a sunbed?
* 20,000 Columbian Peso note in his wallet.
* Irritated by booster jab on left shoulder.

There was precisely a pint of Monkford's blood spilled in the car. Tests showed that the blood had been previously frozen.

Steve Ewa

TEL: 020 7978 18~~
MOB: 0777
EMA~

Janus Cars offered a very special service, giving its clients a new identity and helping them to escape their old life. Sherlock spared no time in revealing the answer on his website.

SOLVED –
Congratulations to Ian Monkford on his relocation to Columbia.

TRANSCRIPT ON LINE TAP: 07796649870

REQUESTED BY: DI LESTRADE
AUTHORISED BY: CHIEF COMMISSIONER BLAND

CALLER: This one's a bit defective, sorry, she's blind. This is a funny one, I'll give you 12 hours.
SHERLOCK: Why are you doing this?
CALLER: I like to watch you dance.

Makeover Queen Connie Prince (48) has been found dead by her brother in the house they shared in Hampstead. It is believed she cut her hand on a rusty nail while gardening and contracted Tetanus.

CALLER: You're enjoying this aren't you? Joining the dots...
Three hours... Boom boom!

TRA

REQ
AUT

48?
She was 54
if she was
a day...

The first suspicious detail
in Connie Prince's death
was the wound on her
hand. It was clean and
fresh — Tetanus takes 8
days to kill, the wound
was far too new for that.

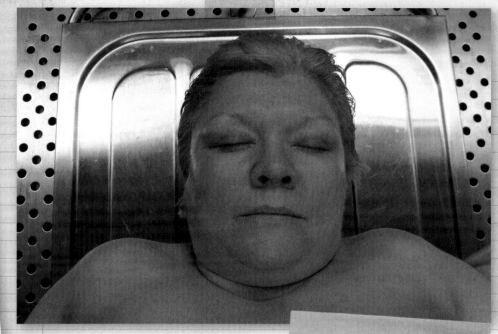

Sherlock was quick to solve the mystery of Connie Prince's death. Raul de Santos, sick of the way Connie treated her brother, his lover, killed her by upping the dose of her Botox injection.

The second time that Botulinum toxin formed a part of these cases.

Are you sure it wasn't the cat?

Perhaps the cat reads your blog and it got ideas.

Shut up about the cat, it was a perfectly valid theory.

You could set up a sister practice, perhaps? John Watson, Pet Policeman.

AULTY GAS MAIN
CAUSES 12 DEATHS

The hostage had broken the rules and people had died. I admit that my faith in Sherlock had been knocked, not because he had failed to solve the problem but because he had failed to grieve.

An explosion rocked a tower block in North Leeds yesterday. Several floors were destroyed with twelve people losing their lives and several more injured. Utility company NorGas insist that the facilities were regularly checked but many are insisting that this is just the latest, tragic event in a history of negligence from the company. ●

Technically, I did solve the case.

Don't make people into heroes, John. Heroes don't exist, and if they did I wouldn't be one of them.

CRIPT O

STED BY: DI LESTRADE
RISED BY: CHIEF COMMISSIONER BLAND

LOCK HOLMES: Hello
       CALLER: Help me!
LOCK HOLMES: Tell us where you are.
       CALLER: His voice... he was so...
LOCK HOLMES: Tell me nothing about him, nothing.
       CALLER: He sounded so soft...

(DISCONNECTED)

The only way forward was forward.

The man was in his late thirties.
He had been dead for around twenty-four hours.
There was considerable bruising around the nose and mouth and he had been in the water some time.

His trousers were heavy-duty, cheap and a size too big. Uniform, then, given to him by his employer. There was a hook on his belt for a walkie-talkie. The soles of his feet and his legs showed he walked a great deal. Yet his backside was flabby so he spent a lot of time sat down too. Security guard.

Badge torn from shirt. He had worked somewhere recognisable. There were crumpled ticket-stubs in his pocket. He worked in a museum or gallery. Hickman Gallery had reported one of their attendants missing: Alex Woodbridge.

The Great Game

Why would a renowned assassin have killed a security guard from the Hickman Gallery? Could it be that he knew something about the Vermeer painting? Perhaps he had proof that it was fake?

The Golem. Where?

VAUXHALL ARCHES

WANTED!

NAME **OSCAR DZUNDA**

ALIAS **THE GOLEM**

Assassin for hire, famous for his method of crushing the life out of his victims with his oversized hands. Originally from the Czech Republic, Dzunda is

Sherlock went to the gallery. I investigated at Alex Woodbridge's flat. An amateur astronomer and professional messer-up of rooms. There was little to discover except for a recorded answer-machine message: 'Alex? It's Professor Cairns, listen, you were right, you were bloody right. Give us a call!'

The picture was a fake, it had to be! But where was the proof? What had Woodbridge discovered?

We tried to catch the Golem at Vauxhall Arches but he ran. Looking up Professor Cairns in the phone directory led us to the London Planetarium.

The Great Game

Unfortunately, the Golem was there too...

We escaped with our lives. Professor Cairns did not. Time was running out.

CCTV2 21:

Professor Cairns at work

LONDON
PLANETAR

Explore
the galaxy...

Back at the gallery and the phone rang. This time the kidnap victim was a child, he counted down from ten, demanding Sherlock prove the Vermeer a fake or lose the challenge.

More than enough time for me, naturally.

It was the Van Buren Supernova, a celestial body that first appeared in 1858 and yet was somehow shown in the sky of a painting allegedly painted in the 1640s. A fact Sherlock picked up from the commentary at the Planetarium. Obviously he didn't know it beforehand, because he knows nothing about astronomy.
Or planets in general.
Or suns. And what goes around them.

No. I only know important things. Like the difference between the ash from a Marlboro Light and that of full tar.

'PRICELE
PAINTIN
FAKE!

We've run out of milk. I used it to grow bacteria.

The Great Game

And still there was the matter of the Bruce Partington plans.
I had investigated on my own. Interviewing Lucy Harrison,
Andrew West's fiancée.

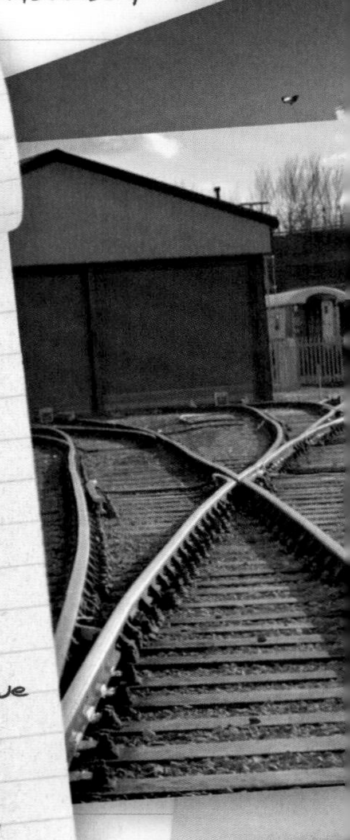

Notes taken following visit to see Lucy Harrison –

* Insistent that Andrew West wouldn't steal.

* I pointed out that he was young, about to get married –
  Lucy said everyone has debts and that West wouldn't
  try to clear them by selling out his country.

* West was unusually quiet on the night of his death.
  He was having a night in with Lucy when out of the blue
  he said he had to go and see someone...

* "He didn't steal those things. Westie was a good man,
  he was my good man..."

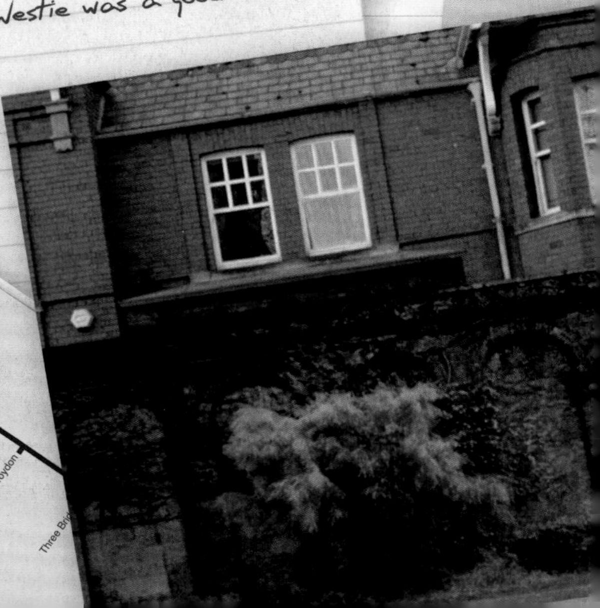

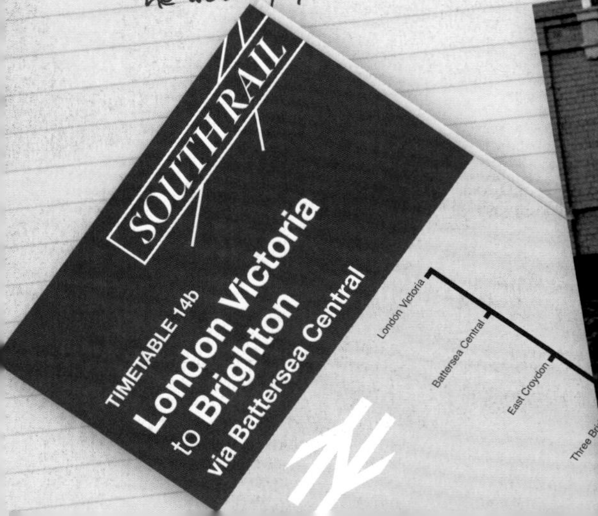

TIMETABLE 14b

SOUTH RAIL

London Victoria
to Brighton
via Battersea Central

London Victoria

Battersea Central

East Croydon

Three Bri

Why was there so little blood on the line? That pointed to the fact that he had died elsewhere, bled out and then been dumped here. But why here?

The points! The reason why Andrew West had no train ticket on him is that he had never got on the train, he was on the roof, his body falling off when the train switched tracks!

Joe Harrison, Lucy's brother. Sold drugs but got out of his depth. Stole the memory stick to make money but Westie caught him out. There was a fight and Westie fell down the steps to Joe's flat. He hit his head and now Joe's looking at a manslaughter charge. So he disposes of the body through the rear window of his flat, right onto the roof of a passing train...

Joe's flat

Battersea →

The Great Game

And of course, Sherlock handed the plans straight back to his brother, didn't he? Didn't he? I mean he wouldn't be so stupid as to use them to try and flush out a psychopath obsessed with destroying him. No. Even Sherlock wouldn't be that reckless, surely?

It worked.

'The Pool' - Sherlock had chosen the place where Carl Powers had died.

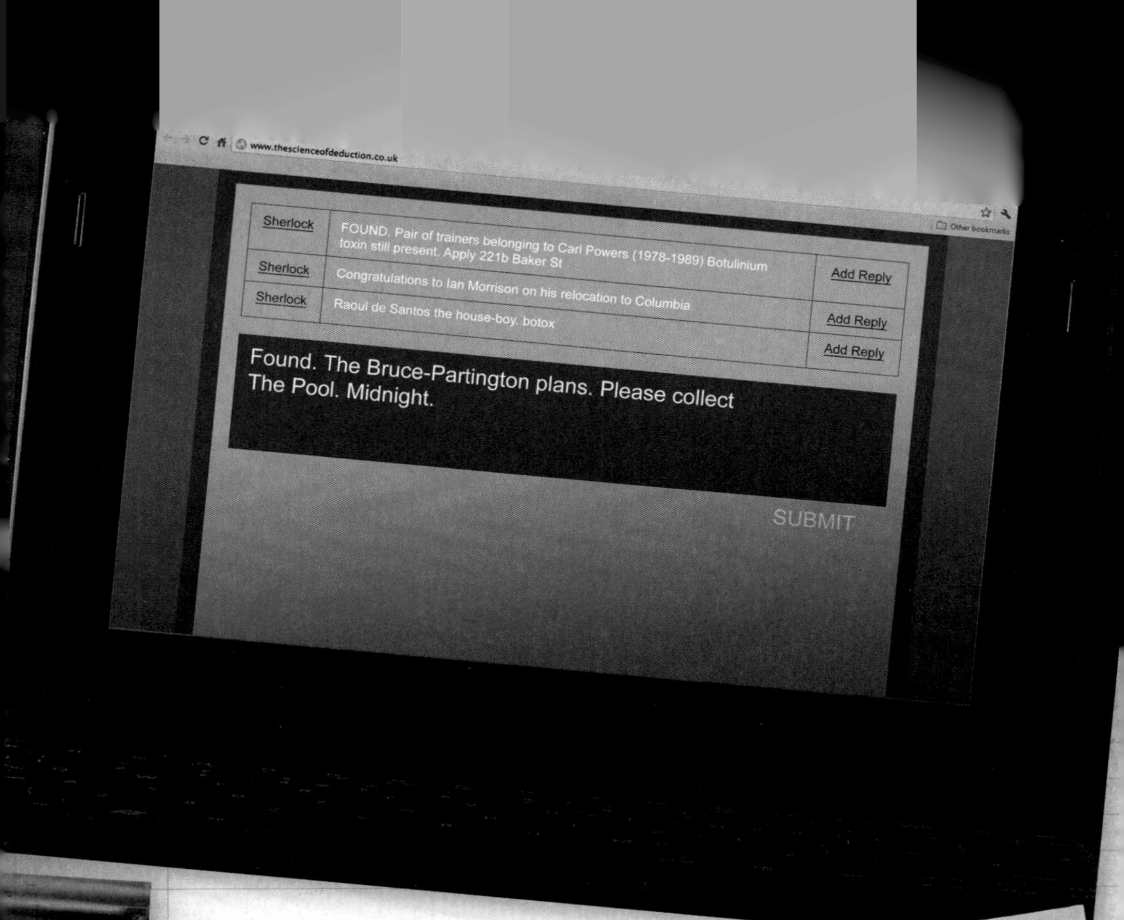

☆ ✎

🗁 Other bookmarks

Sherlock	FOUND. Pair of trainers belonging to Carl Powers (1978-1989) Botulinium toxin still present. Apply 221b Baker St	
Sherlock	Congratulations to Ian Morrison on his relocation to Columbia.	Add Reply
Sherlock	Raoul de Santos the house-boy. botox	Add Reply
		Add Reply

Found. The Bruce-Partington plans. Please collect
The Pool. Midnight.

SUBMIT

It worked? Yes. It worked. In that whole 'being kidnapped, thrown in the back of a van, wired up to a load of explosive and then dumped at the side of a swimming pool with countless sniper-rifles pointing at me before Moriarty disappears anyway so what was the point' sort of way. Yes. Worked really well. Yes. We should definitely do that again.

You've just described one of the best nights of your life and you know it.

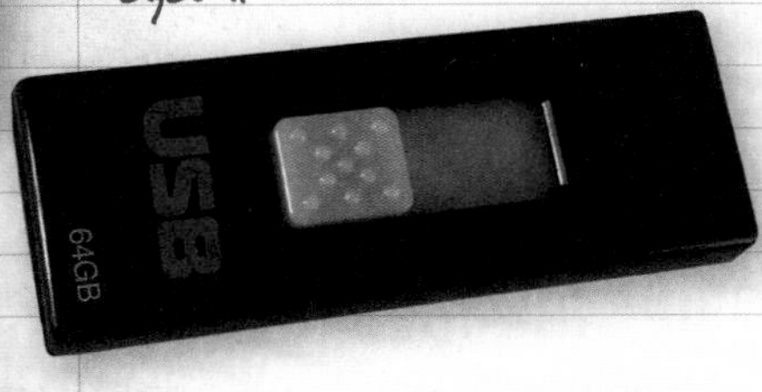

yes.

USB

64GB

THE ADVENTURE OF THE PLAYFUL VILLAIN

he idea of chatting to Moriarty is a daunting one. The conversation would be filled with misdirection and threats of violence. Only a hopeless optimist would expect to survive. Thankfully, the same cannot be said of Andrew Scott, the actor behind the role. Though he confesses we might not be able to trust everything he says. 'It's hard talking about acting,' he admits. 'It's so instinctual. You say all these things, but in the end you feel like adding "or maybe not…"'

He's had to do his fair share of talking, though; his appearance as Holmes's ultimate enemy has guaranteed him a wealth of attention, something Andrew takes in his stride. 'Nothing must overtake the job itself, so the attention can be a bit scary, but Benedict, Martin and I have been around a while – we can see it for what it is.'

Not that Andrew realised what he was getting himself into straight away.

'Well, the character appeared very briefly in the first draft of *The Great Game*, credited as "Jim", and I was reading it very quickly as I was working at the time. It took a while for it to click. "OK, Jim… yeah… right… Oh… Jim *Moriarty*… I see!"'

Once the penny had dropped, did it make him think about other actors who had performed the role?

'I didn't do any research, I just went for it. People always ask, "Have you read this,

have you read that?" and I say, no but I have read the scene seventy-seven times! When something's as well written as this, the script's all you have to think about. It allowed me to be freer in my approach.'

It was certainly a brave, revolutionary take on the role.

'He seemed to me to be very playful. I always think people are at their scariest when they are surprising, when you have no idea what they're going to do. He's a theatrical character. One has to play that truthfully. It could be confused for someone being over the top, but people have the most extreme ways of expressing themselves. It's tempting as an actor to take the safest route, to say your lines and never move your face, but I wanted to show that some people can be extremely dynamic and physical and that there's a psychological motive and a truth to them.'

Moriarty doesn't get much more theatrical than during the last episode of Series Two, *The*

Moriarty is 'totally obsessed' with Sherlock

Andrew Scott as Sherlock's nemesis, Jim Moriarty

Reichenbach Fall, when he's breaking into the Tower of London.

'They were playing the music by Rossini [*La gazza ladra*, or *The Thieving Magpie*] and I just began to dance along, it wasn't scripted. They ended up using quite a lot of it, so that was incredibly enjoyable! Sinister and dark people don't behave in a dark way. They make people around them feel dark and scary but they don't feel that way themselves. They don't walk around in a big black cloak. It was important to me that he was able to wear a grey suit. People worry about that – how can he be the villain if he's wearing a cream tie! The fact that he's Moriarty and that he's done all these terrible things is scary enough.

'When he's in the courtroom [in the same episode], he's very clever. He understands the human condition, he understands that people want to be flattered. Later, having tea with Sherlock, he can reveal himself, he can be as relaxed and flirtatious as he wants. It's a quiet moment but, because it's so well set up and so beautifully written, the inherent threat feels extremely potent.'

All the more so, perhaps, because the relationship between Sherlock and Moriarty is as deep and complex as the relationship between Sherlock and John.

'They're the same person, they've just gone different ways. Moriarty has to match Sherlock, he has to be as intelligent and quick-witted. He has to understand him. He has a total obsession with Sherlock, and I think Sherlock is obsessed with him, too. They need one another. People love the relationship between John and Sherlock because it's about friendship, it's about what it means to love someone else. Moriarty doesn't have any friends, he doesn't have anyone to love, that's why he's become sociopathic.

'I wanted to show little glimpses of Moriarty's vulnerability. You can't go down that road too much because that's not what one's job is when playing the main antagonist, but you got to see that towards the very end, when we realise he's going to kill himself. He's a very desolate, very lonely, very unhappy person.'

The public response to Andrew's portrayal was extremely vocal. Did he expect as much?

'I was a bit naive about how successful it was going to be. It became popular instantly, with both the audience and the critics, so by the time it aired there was a weight of expectation. I hadn't seen the episode – which seems crazy, now I think about it – so I was watching it along with everyone else, worrying what it was going to be like.

'I'm glad that I decided to do whatever I wanted to do, though, and not worry about how popular it was going to be. I had a certain sense that what I was doing was a little bit left of centre but not wilfully so. Of course, certainly in the first series, a few viewers were unsure: "Oh God, no! This isn't the way I want Moriarty to be!" I was prepared for that. It was always going to create an extreme reaction. It was a face they probably didn't associate with a villain – or probably associate with anything for most people. The important thing is, whether some like it or some abhor it, you can't change your performance based on either of those reactions. You have to do what feels right whether there are eight people watching or eight million.' ∎

THE GREAT GAME
BY THE BOOK

VICTORIA REGINA Holmes's habit of indulging in firearms practice during moments of boredom is taken straight from the original stories. In *The Adventure of the Musgrave Ritual*, Watson notes that 'pistol practice should distinctly be an open-air pastime; and when Holmes in one of his queer humours would sit in an arm-chair, with his hair trigger and a hundred Boxer cartridges, and proceed to adorn the opposite wall with a patriotic V.R. done in bullet-pocks, I felt strongly that neither the atmosphere nor the appearance of our room was improved by it.' V.R. stood for *Victoria Regina*, Latin for 'Victoria reigns'.

As Victoria no longer reigns (and Sherlock's sympathies are perhaps a little less royalist in inclination), he opts for a simple smiley face these days (and one painted in the same hue of paint used by the Tong in the previous episode).

MY BRAIN IS MY HARD-DRIVE!
'Something I was determined to get across in *The Great Game*,' says writer Mark Gatiss, 'is that Sherlock is also spectacularly ignorant.'

Doyle had written a conversation very similar to Sherlock and John's regarding the detective's lack of astronomical knowledge. 'What the deuce is it to me?' Holmes had blustered when called on the fact, 'you say that we go around the sun. If we went around the moon it would not make a pennyworth of difference to me or my work.'

'I love that,' says Mark, 'and the explanation – the idea that if he puts superfluous knowledge in his head he'll run out of room for the important things!'

I'D BE LOST WITHOUT MY BLOGGER
In the first Holmes short story, *A Scandal in Bohemia*, Holmes comments that he would be 'lost without his Boswell', referring to James Boswell, the famous biographer of Samuel Johnson.

THE BRUCE-PARTINGTON PLANS
'The Adventure of the Bruce-Partington Plans', originally published in 1912, is followed closely throughout *The Great Game*, albeit with a lot of tweaks to bring it up to date. In the original story, Mycroft wants Holmes to trace the plans to the Bruce-Partington submarine (rather than a missile), and naturally they are hard copy as opposed to data files on a memory stick. Still, the main suspect is found beside the rail tracks,

and the body found itself there via much the same method. In *The Great Game*, Westie's murderer is Joe Harrison, the name lifted from a similar story, 'The Adventure of the Naval Treaty'.

THE FIVE PIPS
In 'The Five Orange Pips', Holmes investigates the case of a man who is sent five dried orange pips through the post. It's a warning, much as the Greenwich pips are here.

YOU SEE BUT YOU DO NOT OBSERVE
Holmes gives exactly this advice to Lestrade in 'A Scandal in Bohemia', too.

ANY SPARE CHANGE?
'They're on every street corner,' says Mark Gatiss. 'They're like CCTV, living cameras.' Where Doyle's Holmes used his Baker Street Irregulars, a ragtag bunch of street urchins, Sherlock has his homeless network. Both can pass unseen through the London streets gathering information for their employer. ■

VAUXHALL ARCHES

STEEL TRUE, BLADE STRAIGHT

'If in one hundred years I am only known as the man who invented Sherlock Holmes, then I will have considered my life a failure.'
– Sir Arthur Conan Doyle

Born into a large family in Edinburgh, Sir Arthur Ignatius Conan Doyle's childhood was one of penury and frequent rows. His father was a chronic alcoholic and the young Doyle escaped into fiction, later recalling the soothing effect of the stories his mother used to tell: 'In my early childhood, as far as I can remember anything at all, the vivid stories she would tell me stand out so clearly that they obscure the real facts of my life.'

At the age of nine, wealthy members of his extended family agreed to pay for his studies and he was sent to England where he boarded at a strict Jesuit school. He hated every moment of it but worked hard, graduating at seventeen. 'Perhaps it was good for me that the times were hard,' he later wrote, 'for I was wild, full blooded and a trifle reckless. But the situation called for energy and application so that one was bound to try to meet it. My mother had been so splendid that I could not fail her.'

On his return to Edinburgh, one of the first things he did was co-sign the committal papers that would send his father into the care of a lunatic asylum.

His mother had been forced to take lodgers in order to make ends meet, and one of them was to have a profound influence on Doyle. While most of his family had followed careers in the arts, Bryan Charles Waller, a young doctor, inspired Doyle in a different direction. Waller encouraged Doyle to train at the medical school in Edinburgh where the young man would meet Dr Joseph Bell, a tutor whose deductive process and frequent eccentricity was to be a major influence on the character of Sherlock Holmes.

Doyle wrote his first story while training, 'The Mystery of Sasassa Valley', which owed a debt to Edgar Allan Poe and Bret Harte, his favourite writers at the time. It was published in a local magazine, *Chamber's Journal*, which had also published Thomas Hardy's first writing. His second story, 'The American Tale', was published in *London Society* a few months later.

During his third year of training, he was offered a post as ship's doctor on the whaling vessel *Hope*. Unable to resist such an adventurous prospect, he took the job and, despite some reservations about the brutality of the work conducted by the crew, he greatly enjoyed his time traversing the Arctic. He returned to his training the following year with reluctance.

After graduating, he took a job on a steamer that travelled between Liverpool and Africa, hoping to rekindle the adventure of his time aboard the *Hope*. Sadly, he hated it and resigned his post as quickly as possible. Close

The mighty Sir Arthur Conan Doyle

felt it offered the perfect terrain. Encouraging two locals to join him, they practised at night to avoid ridicule. 'I am convinced,' he wrote, 'that the time will come when hundreds of Englishmen will come to Switzerland for the skiing season.' He was, of course, quite right.

In 1885, he married Louisa Hawkins and continued to balance his life between his medical practice and his urge to write. The following year, he began work on a short novel, 'A Tangled Skein', which featured the adventures of a consulting detective by the name of Sheridan Hope and his doctor friend Ormond Sacker. By 1888, this had become *A Study in Scarlet*, and the characters' names had changed to Sherlock Holmes and Dr John Watson. Published in *Beeton's Christmas Annual*, it was a popular success though Doyle was more satisfied with his next novel, *Micah Clark* which few have ever heard of.

Doyle's writing was particularly well received in America and, in 1889, he was invited to dinner by Joseph Marshall Stoddart, the publisher of the successful, Philadelphia-based magazine *Lippincott's Monthly*. Doyle's fellow guest at the meal was Oscar Wilde and the two extremely different men got on rather well, each enjoying the other's company and agreeing to contribute material to a planned UK version of Stoddart's magazine.

Wilde was commissioned to write *The Picture of Dorian Gray*; Doyle's contribution was to be a second Holmes novel, *The Sign of Four*. In order to fulfil the commission, he had to set aside his novel *The White Company*, which he always considered his best work. Though it would soon be published, it received none of the accolade and attention that the Holmes stories did and the formula for the rest of his creative life was set: editors and readers wanted Sherlock Holmes; Doyle wanted to be

to bankruptcy, he moved to Portsmouth and set himself up as a General Practitioner. Only able to furnish two rooms of the house he lived in (the rooms his patients would see), he worked hard over the following three years to increase his standing and, eventually, built up a solvent practice.

Doyle was a keen sportsman, playing as goalkeeper for Portsmouth Association Football Club, an amateur side that existed prior to the current Portsmouth team. He also played cricket for the Marylebone Cricket Club and once bowled out cricketing legend W.G. Grace. One of the first people to take up the sport of skiing, he discovered it in Norway and then travelled to Switzerland because he a 'serious' writer and embark on new work. It was an imbalance that would plague him for the rest of his life.

Doyle set up a practice in London which, according to his autobiography at least, never received a single client. Taking advantage of the time this allowed him to write, he made the practical decision to write a series of Holmes stories for *The Strand* magazine. These were phenomenally successful and Doyle finally decided that he would abandon his attempts at a medical career and concentrate solely on writing.

Between 1891 and 1893, Doyle wrote twenty-four Holmes stories, finally killing the character off in 'The Adventure of the Final Problem'. Doyle was bored by Holmes and desperately wanted to move on. He created an arch-enemy in the form of Professor Moriarty, the 'Napoleon of Crime', and had Holmes

sacrifice himself by wrestling the criminal genius off a mountain path and plunging into the Reichenbach Falls in Switzerland. As a result, *The Strand* lost twenty thousand subscribers. Doyle cared not one jot, throwing himself into new projects. In fact, he became so blinded by his new literary efforts that he failed to notice the decline in health of his wife. By the time her illness had become obvious, there was nothing that could be done. Louisa was diagnosed with tuberculosis and given a few months to live. Doyle refused to accept this and ministered to her night and day. She survived for a number of years, but their relationship was now one of doctor and patient rather than husband and wife.

Depressed at his wife's illness and later the death of his father, Doyle began to immerse himself in the study of the occult. He had always been interested in the subject but it was soon to dominate his life. He joined the Society of Psychical Research and became heavily interested in spiritualism.

The famous illustration of Holmes and Moriarty's final battle

In the spring of 1897, he met Jean Leckie, a 24-year-old mezzo-soprano whose family claimed to be descendants of the Scottish hero Rob Roy. Doyle fell in love but refused to act on it out of respect for his wife, who was still alive against all odds. Despite this, Doyle and Jean remained close and would eventually have their day, marrying ten years later.

Sherlock Holmes was to raise his head once more before the nineteenth century was out. Needing an income and knowing only one sure way to do so, Doyle wrote a stage play featuring the character. William Gillette, a renowned American actor, loved the script but asked for permission to revise

William Gillette's production of Sherlock Holmes

it. Famously, Doyle gave a suitably careless response: 'You may marry him, murder him or do anything you like to him.' Gillette went on to rewrite the play extensively and it toured the USA to great success, opening in London in 1901. The UK critics were not kind in their opinions, but people went anyway and it was a great success.

Meanwhile, Doyle had volunteered to serve in the Boer War, determined that, having written about it but never experienced it first hand, he should do his duty and fight for his country. He was deemed too unfit so he enlisted as an army doctor instead. He would spend several months in Africa, watching more troops meet their deaths through typhoid than enemy action. He wrote an epic, 500-page treatise on the war and returned to England despondent and directionless.

He tried his hands at politics, running for the Central Edinburgh seat. He lost by a narrow margin and returned to London and Sherlock Holmes. The detective that continued to plague Doyle returned to print in a serialised novel set before the character's death. *The Hound of the Baskervilles* would go on to be the most famous and well-regarded Holmes tale of them all. Doyle gave in completely soon afterwards, devising a method for his character to have escaped death and writing new stories for *The Strand* to begin serialising in 1903.

In 1906, Louisa finally died, breathing her last while held in Doyle's arms, a full thirteen years after she had been diagnosed. Doyle sank into another bout of depression, attempting to distract himself by becoming involved with some detective work of his own. A young half-Indian lawyer called George Edalji had been convicted of writing threatening letters and mutilating horses and cows. Despite the fact that the mutilations continued after Edalji was imprisoned and the young man's eyesight was so bad he couldn't have committed the attack anyway, Doyle had a fight on his hands to have the case overturned. He was eventually successful, and the affair formed the basis of Julian Barnes's 2005 novel *Arthur and George*.

The following year, Doyle finally married Jean Leckie and began a period of contentment unlike any other during his life. He had had two children with Louisa and he moved them, along with Jean, out of London to a cottage in Sussex where he devoted his

SP

time to writing – mostly unsuccessful – plays. As had happened so often before, he returned to Holmes once the bank account was lean and produced a theatrical version of his short story 'The Adventure of the Speckled Band'. The play was successful though it fell foul of an old acting adage: never work with children or animals. Doyle had insisted that the production use a real snake, overruling the actors and crew in the decision. He was eventually forced to admit this had been a mistake: 'The Python either hung down like a pudgy yellow bell rope, or else when his tail was pinched, endeavoured to squirm back and get level with the stage carpenter who pinched him, which was not in the script.'

Aside from plays and the science fiction novel *The Lost World*, which introduced his other well-known hero, Professor Challenger, he produced mainly children, two sons Denis and Adrian and another daughter, Jean. Life was good.

Then the First World War hit and life changed again. Doyle tried to enlist but, at 55, was too old for a soldier's duty. He instead dedicated himself to organising a civilian battalion and offering naval suggestions to the War Office to provide inflatable life boats and belts to their sailors or body armour to soldiers on the front line. The suggestions were treated as the work of a pest by most, though Winston Churchill took the time to thank him for the ideas.

One of the hoax images made of the 'Cottingley Fairies'

himself a powerful medium and achieved all of his tricks by supernatural means. This led to a very public disagreement, with Doyle branding Houdini a 'dangerous enemy'.

During the conflict, Doyle lost his son, his brother, two brothers in law and both his nephews. In 1919, he turned to spiritualism once more. It came to almost entirely occupy his life and for the next seven years he wrote little fiction, preferring to write about esoteric matters. He channelled a quarter of a million pounds into research, encouraged Jean to develop the 'skill' of trance-writing and famously lent his support to the Cottingley Fairies, a series of photographs claiming to depict fairies that were later proved to be (unknown to Doyle) a hoax. After a string of non-fiction books and articles, he returned to fiction, albeit with a hefty spiritualist theme, writing the Professor Challenger novel *The Land of Mist*. Sadly, this deepening faith in

supernatural matters cost him his friendship with escapologist and magician Harry Houdini. Houdini grew to become a vocal opponent of spiritualism, using his skills and techniques to expose fraudulent mediums and psychics. Unable to accept the evidence, Doyle insisted that Houdini was

By the end of the decade, his own death hung close. He went on one last 'psychic tour' in 1929, travelling through Holland, Denmark, Sweden and Norway. Already diagnosed with Angina Pectoris, the physical exertion took its toll and he was bedridden on his return to England. He made one last break for freedom, sneaking unseen from his bed to take a walk in the garden. He was found later, lying on his back clutching at his heart; in his other hand he held a single white snowdrop. Carried back to his bed, he died some weeks later, his final words uttered to his wife. 'You are wonderful,' he told her before slipping away. ∎

Doyle's final resting place in Minstead, Hampshire

THE ADVENTURE OF THE OVERNIGHT SUCCESS

'T'he show was such a big success that it was ridiculous,' laughs Steven Moffat. 'This was our pet project that's all, a vanity project even… Now it's huge.'

As soon as the first series ended, audiences and reviewers were clamouring for more, lamenting the fact that there had 'only' been three episodes.

The second series adapted Doyle's *A Scandal in Bohemia*

'There just aren't enough months in the year to make more,' says Mark Gatiss. 'These three episodes are three, full-on movies and take a lot of time and effort to produce.'

'We want each one to feel special,' Steven agrees, 'to look beautiful and feel like an event.'

An event certainly, with Steven and Mark deciding to tackle the three most famous stories: 'A Scandal in Bohemia', with the woman who beat Sherlock Holmes, *The Hound of the Baskervilles*, the most filmed adventure of them all, and 'The Final Problem', with Holmes appearing to go to his death in order to rid the world of Moriarty.

'Why defer the pleasure?' asks Steven. 'There are plenty of places to go after these stories, plenty more adventures to see. These are still the early days of our hero's career.'

And it's a career that has come on apace since last we saw Sherlock and John. John's blog, once just a therapeutic aid, is now famed worldwide and Sherlock has as many fans in the fictional world of the show as he does in real life. Though at least they seem content to let him walk down the street unmolested, which was more of a challenge when it came to the actual filming with crowds of people turning up outside the fictional 221B, hoping to catch informative glimpses.

As the series progresses, John and Sherlock develop a strong friendship...

'It was like street theatre,' admits Benedict Cumberbatch. 'Hundreds of people standing across the road from you while you try and get the shot.'

Half of the internet caught fire once Twitter started discussing the sight of Lara Pulver, as Irene Adler, wearing Sherlock's dressing gown. The other half is sure to ignite once filming starts for Series Three.

Not only has Sherlock's career improved but so has his relationship with his flatmate.

'They've moved on,' Benedict says. 'While there will always be things about each other that they dislike, they've grown closer. They've become real friends.'

'And we get to show them having fun!' adds Steven. 'A pair of naughty schoolboys.'

'You can't stay still,' says Mark. 'The characters have to move on.'

If John was still baffled by everything and Sherlock was still the coldest fish in the ocean, we the audience would certainly wonder whether the two of them had been spending any time with one another over the intervening months. These are the two friends who complete one another, who fix one another and by the time we meet them again they are clearly stronger. And they'll need to be to face the Woman, the hound and the fall... ∎

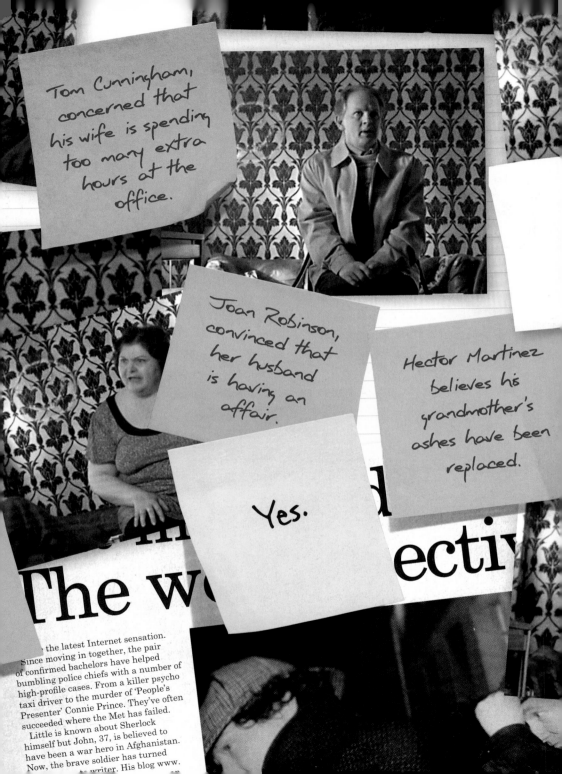

Tom Cunningham, concerned that his wife is spending too many extra hours at the office.

Joan Robinson, convinced that her husband is having an affair.

Hector Martinez believes his grandmother's ashes have been replaced.

Yes.

The we

ectiv

the latest Internet sensation. Since moving in together, the pair of confirmed bachelors have helped bumbling police chiefs with a number of high-profile cases. From a killer psycho taxi driver to the murder of 'People's Presenter' Connie Prince. They've often succeeded where the Met has failed.

Little is known about Sherlock himself but John, 37, is believed to have been a war hero in Afghanistan. Now, the brave soldier has turned writer. His blog www.

BORING!

Debra and Maria Wilkinson, refused access to their grandfather after he had died.

Leonard Cummins (and entourage), hopeful that Sherlock could retrieve a stolen computer database containing important 'business' information.

FLYAWAY AIRLINE

Name of passenger:
JOHN CONISTON

Seat number:
11B

Gate:
A

Flight number:
007

Destination:
BERLIN

Remarks / Observations:

PLEASE RETAIN THIS PART OF YOUR TICKET THROUGH

Lestrade brought us in on the discovery of a body in a car boot in Southwark. A body belonging to a man who, according to his passport and boarding pass, should have been involved in a German plane crash the day before.

A hiker, Charles McCarthy, was found dead from a single blow to the back of the head with a blunt instrument.

The body was found by Bill Crowder, a salesman for animal food products.

Perhaps he ate his own stock while on the road.

Crowder had been stuck in the valley after his car stalled. He had spotted McCarthy, standing next to the stream and looking up into the sky. Crowder's car backfired, distracting him. When he looked back, McCarthy was dead.

McCarthy was an experienced sportsman recently returned from foreign travel, that much was clear to Sherlock from a glance. So what had killed him?

The sound of the car backfiring had distracted McCarthy. He had been looking up into the sky as he had just thrown a boomerang that he had brought back from his travels. Turning to look at the car, the boomerang had hit him on the back of his head before falling into the stream and being washed away. Simple.

Simple for me. The rest of you monkeys were scratching your heads as usual.

CASE NOTES:

A Scandal in Belgravia

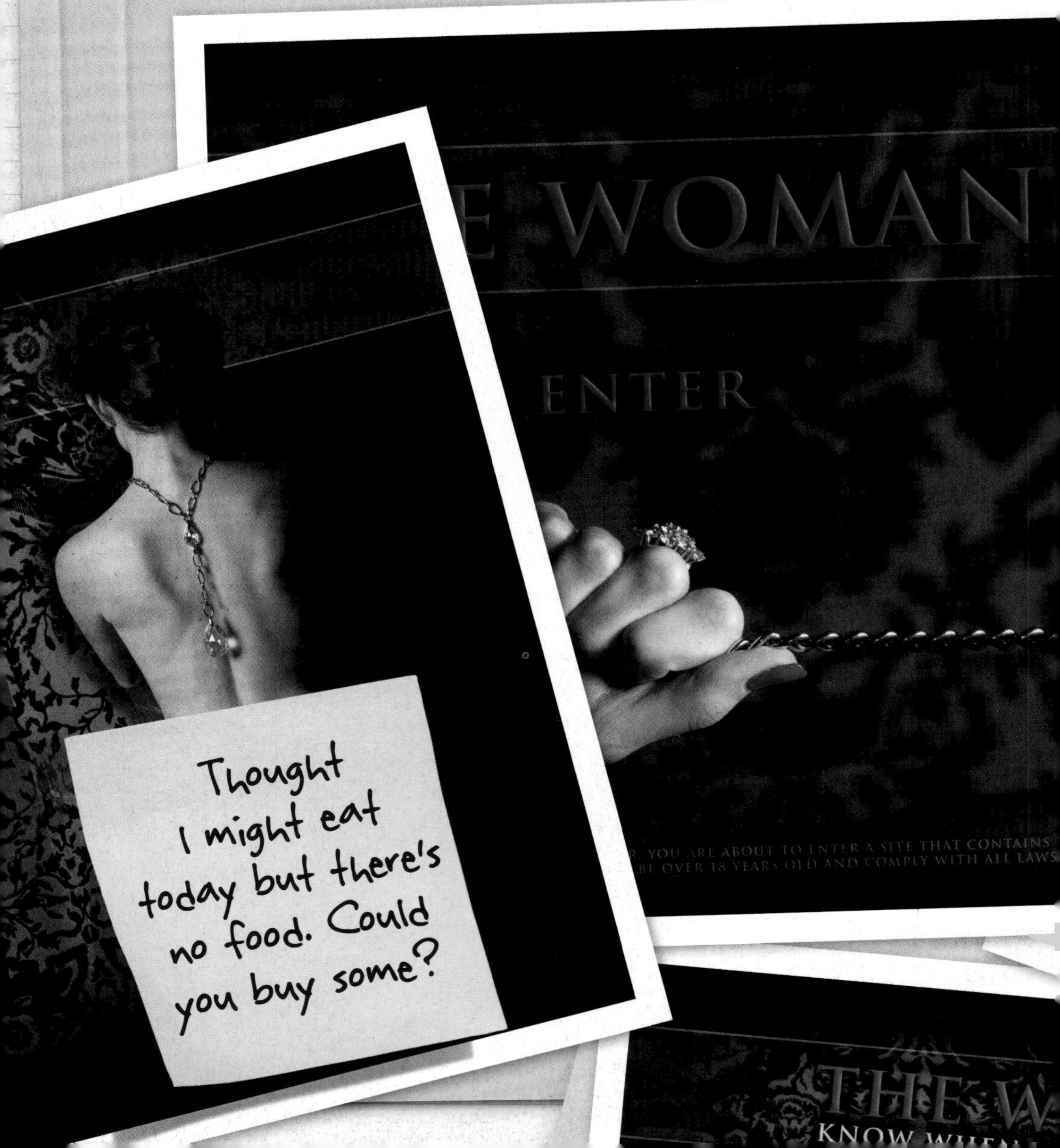

THE WOMAN

KNOW WHEN YOU ARE BEATEN

HOME   SESSIONS   CONTACT   JOIN

EVERY FANTASY.

EVERY SHUDDER OF EXCITEMENT.

EVERY DIRTY LITTLE SECRET.

THE WOMAN.

THE WO

KNOW WHEN YOU AR

HOME   SESSIONS   CONTA

SOME ARE BORN TO RULE

SOME ARE FORCED TO SERVE

WHEN YOU WORSHIP AT THE FEET OF THE
YOU'LL BE IN THE PRESENCE OF YOUR GO

YOU'LL WHIMPER, YOU'LL CRY, YOU'LL FEEL EV
- PHYSICALLY AND MENTALLY.

YOU WILL KNOW WHEN YOU ARE BEATEN.

MAN
BEATEN

A Scandal in Belgravia

Sherlock had been busy for months, his new-found fame bringing lots of clients to our door.

Then, finally, a rather more illustrious client came knocking. With security staff and a private helicopter.

Boring clients wanting me to solve boring problems. Idiots. Jilted lovers. Inept boomerang operators. I loathed the lot of them.

How easily you are impressed. If he'd been wearing a big shiny uniform, would you have asked if he could be your best friend?

We agreed I don't get out of bed for less than a seven.

Despite our client's location, I had no way of judging how interesting the case would be at that point. It was a point of principle.

I was flown to a rather well-known address.

Sherlock was there. Wrapped in nothing but his bed sheet. Obviously.

According to Mycroft, Irene Adler (a ~~famous dominatrix known as 'the Woman'~~) possessed compromising photos of ~~one of~~ the royal family. He wanted Sherlock to retrieve them.

Can you feel that, John? Like the brush of silk on the back of your neck? That is the attention of the SAS, John, the delicate touch of rifle crosshairs.

Please remove all this material as Mrs Hudson will have the unpleasant task of cleaning brain matter from the pile of your terrible hearthrug.

We went to Miss Adler's house. Sherlock was going to pretend to be a vicar who had been in a fight. Which sounds SO stupid when you write it down.

I would be an eyewitness who tagged along to help. At the earliest opportunity I would set off the fire alarm so that Adler would give away the location of the photos. Needless to say it didn't go according to plan. In fact, within five minutes I was on my knees with a gun to my head. Again.

You didn't complain at the time.

I was too busy applying your make-up. And loving it.

I saved you all, didn't I?

AND got the phone with the compromising images on it.

For all of five minutes, yes. Then you got yourself whipped, drugged and dumped by a woman, naked except for your coat. I've still not forgiven you.

A Scandal in Belgravia

And for a while all we heard from Irene Adler was the sound of her sighing. Over and over again. Having personalised her text alert on Sherlock's phone. It was like she'd moved in.

You're exaggerating.
It didn't happen that often.

57 times in the run-up to Christmas. Your pocket was moaning more than Mrs Hudson.

Thank you for that mental image.

Dearest Sherlock
Love Molly xxx

To my lovely boys

Hope the next year brings you all the dead bodies and things you like,

Mrs Hudson
x

Then, Christmas festivities took a darker turn. Sherlock received a gift from Adler – her phone, security locked.

Sherlock contacted Mycroft, telling him that Irene Adler's dead body would soon be found.

Sherlock was called to St. Barts to identify what may have been Adler.

He confirmed it was.

FORENSIC REPORT

REPORT BY: Molly Hooper

NOTES:

The body was brought in via government channels, having been found in Regent's Park. Initially labelled as a Jane Doe, she was later identified by Sherlock Holmes as being someone. I'm not sure who exactly because, of course, nobody would tell me. He managed to identify her by her naked body rather than her face (which was extremely damaged after repeated beating with a blunt object). I don't know how because ~~Sherlock Mr Holmes doesn't normally~~ It was probably something he noticed, a freckle or stain or something. He's very clever like that. He notices things. Most things. Just not BLOODY PEOPLE.

A Scandal in Belgravia

But Adler didn't stay dead long...

And, just in case it looked like we were going to have a quiet New Year's Eve, we had a visit from a CIA hit squad to liven things up a bit. They made the mistake of attacking Mrs Hudson.

Who later took great pleasure in wiping the worst offender's blood and spittle off the bathroom windowsill.

CRIME IN PROGRESS
PLEASE DISTURB

CONFIDENTIAL

TELEPHONE CALL TRANSCRIPT

NUMBER: 0207 646 7803 — DI GREG LESTRADE DIRECT LINE

CALLER: Lestrade? We've had a break-in at Baker Street. Send your least irritating officers and an ambulance. Oh, no, we're fine. No, it's the burglar, he's got himself rather badly injured. Oh, a few broken ribs, fractured skull, suspected punctured lung... He fell out of a window.

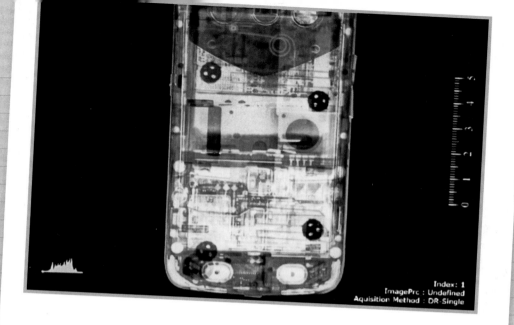

Index: 1
ImagePrc : Undefined
Aquisition Method : DR-Single

Meanwhile, when he wasn't playing Bin Skittles with Americans, Sherlock continued to investigate Adler's phone.

He noticed via an X-Ray that it was primed with explosive, small charges that would destroy the phone's memory if it were tampered with. The only way to gain access to its contents was to enter the four-digit passcode.

Something he kept failing to do.

WRONG PASSCO
I AM
2 2 1 B
LOCKED
2 ATTEMPTS
REMAINING

Did you ever doubt I'd solve it?

I've never doubted you'd solve anything.

A Scandal in Belgravia

As if we weren't enjoying ourselves enough we were lucky to end up with Adler as a houseguest. On the run from 'killers' (that's as specific as she got, being as forthcoming as ever) she broke in and asked for Sherlock's help to decode an email she had copied from one of her clients.

Sherlock figured it out at breakneck speed. No doubt having a woman to impress helped.

I didn't need to impress her, she would hardly have asked for my help unless she was already in awe of me.

Subject: 007

From: **Chris Stuart** <c.stuart@mod.co.uk>
29 November 2010 11:23:45 CEST
To: Miles Cottrell <m.cottrell@mod.co.uk>
Reply-To: c.stuart@mod.co.uk

007 Confirmed allocation.

42C12C45F13E13G60A60B61F34G34J60D12H33K34K
****
****

Seating plan of the 747 flight to Baltimore.

The numbers were plane seats. Sometimes in small batches where people were sitting next to each other. The plane was wide enough for a 'k' seat, so it was a jumbo. There was a row 13, which also narrowed it down as some flight companies are too superstitious to use one. If 007 was the flight number — and Clever Old Sherlock assured us it was — then that narrowed it down even more. Assuming a British point of origin and the fact that the flight must be scheduled in the near future... Sherlock decided it was a Baltimore flight from Heathrow scheduled to leave at half six the following day.

Simple.

Simple, he says, it still makes my brain hurt.

Each to his own, I couldn't remove a man's kidney. Well, I probably could ...

Unfortunately, the fact that Miss Adler immediately decided to share all this with Jim Moriarty didn't help matters between Sherlock and his brother. Nothing would help matters there. Short of assassination.

Sherlock received tickets for the Baltimore flight and a summons from Mycroft.

FLYAWAY AIRLINES

Y AIRLINES

From:
LHR

To:
BWI

Name of passenger:
SHERLOCK HOLM

nger:

OCK HOLMES

Seat number:
1B

Gate:
xxx

Departure time:
****** 18:30

Destination:

Flight number:

Destination:
BALTIMO

A Scandal in Belgravia

Sherlock remembered part of a call he had heard Mycroft make: "Bond air is a go, that's decided. Check with the Coventry lot". Sherlock began to piece together the secret of flight 007.

The British and American secret services had intercepted plans for a bomb to be placed on the plane. Rather than reveal that they had access to such information, they planned to let the flight go ahead, like the story of the Coventry bombings during the Second World War.

Debra and Maria Wilkinson, refused access to their grandfather after he had died.

Unsolved cases

But Mycroft had come up with a perfect solution. All of the passengers on the plane had been replaced with dead bodies, the absence of which had been hinted at by a number of our clients. But we had missed the pattern. When the flight took off it would be unmanned but, after the bomb had been triggered, there would appear to have been hundreds of casualties.

The terrorists would have been content, confident that their plan had worked. The secret services of two different countries would have still been able to utilise their asset to secure information.

Then Sherlock happened.

FLYAWAY AIRLINES

Name of passenger:

JOHN CONISTON

Seat number:

11B

Gate:

A

Flight number:

007

Destination:

BERLIN

Remarks / Observations:

PLEASE RETAIN THIS PART ... CKET THROUGHOUT YOUR FLIGHT

Hector Martinez believes his grandmother's ashes have been replaced.

I AM SHER LOCKED

12:14

Messages   The Woman   Ed

Text Message

Even you have got to eat.
Let's have dinner.

BBC1 right now. You'll
laugh.

I'm thinking of sending you
a Christmas present.

Mantelpiece

31 Dec 2010 10:34

I'm not dead. Let's have
dinner.

Happy New Year. SH

Goodbye Mr Holmes

Text Message   Send

FREQUENT FLYER #

It seemed that Adler was indeed the woman who had beaten Sherlock Holmes.

For all of half an hour at least. That's how long it took him to deduce the passcode for the phone. Adler had been full of demands, money and protection, secure in the knowledge that nobody would ever access the information on the phone unless she wished them to. She was, of course, wrong.

She was eventually entered into a witness protection programme in America, where no doubt she flourishes to this day.

No doubt.

Air A

ARDING PASS
OLMES/SHERLOC

ROM:
LONDON - LHR

TO:
KARACHI - KHI

VERTU

' - TOP SECRET

THE ADVENTURE OF 'THE WOMAN'

And we begin with *A Scandal in Belgravia*, and the closest *Sherlock* is ever likely to get to a love story for its titular hero. A love story with betrayal, sexual violence, assassins and a plane full of corpses. We've all been there.

But before we even get to Irene Adler we have the resolution to the previous series' cliffhanger. Returning to the swimming pool in Bedminster, Bristol, the cast and crew were faced with the difficulty of recreating shots

How do you get out of that one?

that they had completed over eighteen months previously.

'We had no way of knowing if we were going to get the second series,' says Mark Gatiss, 'so we couldn't shoot extra at the time.'

Not that they knew back then how they were going to get out of the problem the script set – Steven Moffat had decided he'd cross that bridge when he came to it. The eventual answer was obvious. It was the theme to 1983's dancetastic John Travolta movie *Staying Alive*.

The idea for Moriarty's grotesque (and yet thematically appropriate) ringtone actually came from Sue Vertue, who recalled hearing of a funeral when someone had forgotten to switch their phone to silent thereby subjecting the gathered mourners to an ill-timed dose of Bee Gees. When considering which spectacularly misplaced ringtone would best suit the moment in the script, Sue's story was remembered and the decision made. Trying to disguise the fluctuating haircuts of their lead actors over an eighteen-month gap was far from the most complex problem faced by the crew. During their London recording days they had the small matter of riots to contend with.

Filming one of the final scenes of the episode, the rain-soaked meeting between John and Mycroft in the café beneath 221B, they had already been warned by the police that things could be difficult. The riots took place over five nights in early August. Many cities experienced trouble, but London was the focus of what began as a demonstration against a police shooting and became a free-for-all of looting and destruction.

'They told us we couldn't have any night shoots,' remembers Mark, 'and we were racing to get everything finished in case things took a turn for the worse.'

Which they did. The external filming was fine but, for the scene inside the café, Mark recalls how the rain machine outside the window was suddenly turned off as the first assistant director came running in.

'He just said "Go!" and we all fled!'

The story features an idea inspired by a deleted scene from 1969's James Bond movie *On Her Majesty's Secret Service*, though in the movie it was an underground train the secret service filled with the dead rather than a jumbo jet. The filming of the long, eight-minute scene where Sherlock and Mycroft confront one another onboard the 'Plane of the Dead' proved somewhat trying. Not only was it the last scene of a long night shoot, but the extras employed to play corpses had a habit of falling asleep and snoring or shifting in their seats.

Actor Lara Pulver was fresh from her stint in the BBC One series *Spooks*. Back at home in Los Angeles, she read the script and was so taken with the role of Irene Adler that she recorded a video audition immediately and won the part. She discussed the relationship between Adler and Sherlock with journalist Morgan Jeffery saying: 'It's like they're looking in a mirror at each other. They're just in tune –

Irene Adler – a completely new challenge for Sherlock...

they get each other. They see each other and I think they see through each other's masks.

'Irene wears her mask so well – this powerful dominatrix – and he sees through it. And she does [the same] with him. It's an infatuation. A mutual infatuation.'

An infatuation that caused some small amount of flak after the episode was screened, as one frequently outraged tabloid claimed the broadcast of a naked (though never actually fully seen) Lara Pulver contravened broadcasting standards, since it was shown before the nine o'clock watershed. Of course, the paper handily reproduced the scenes in question so we could all be outraged again over our breakfast. ∎

A SCANDAL IN BELGRAVIA
BY THE BOOK

IT WAS A VERY GOOD YEAR For many fans of Sherlock Holmes, 1895 is his very best year, filled with the most interesting cases. Vincent Starret, journalist and writer of many works on or featuring Holmes, certainly thought so and made reference to as much in his poem *221B*: 'though the world may explode, these two survive / and it is always eighteen ninety-five'. John's broken blog counter in *A Scandal in Belgravia* ensures this remains the case for our modern-day Sherlock.

THE GEEK INTERPRETATION The opening section of the episode is filled with throwaway references to other stories. 'The Geek Interpreter' is a pun on 'The Adventure of the Greek Interpreter'. 'The Speckled Blonde' refers to 'The Adventure of the Speckled Band', and 'the Navel Treatment' is a play on 'The Adventure of the Naval Treaty'.

THE HAT Well, it had to happen. The image of Sherlock Holmes is inextricably linked with a Deerstalker hat. First mentioned in 'The Boscombe Valley Mystery', it was when illustrator Sidney Paget elected to put him in one when illustrating 'The Adventure of Silver Blaze' that it become thoroughly entrenched in the minds of the public. Paget was working on Doyle's description of Holmes's 'sharp, eager face framed in his ear-flapped travelling cap'. As for Sherlock's confusion over what sort of hat it is, obviously it was designed to be worn when stalking deer. Sometimes these clever people can be rather dim.

THE AFFAIR OF THE VATICAN
CAMEOS This is another of those cases that Doyle mentions in passing (this time in *The Hound of the Baskervilles*) but we never actually see. Clearly Sherlock shouts it in this instance to clue John in as to what he is about to do.

A CLERICAL ERROR The story of *A Scandal in Belgravia* sticks fairly closely to its source matter for the opening half of the episode. 'A Scandal in Bohemia' features an adventuress who has a compromising photo (albeit a far milder one). Holmes is hired by someone who initially tries to hide their identity (though the line 'I am accustomed to have mystery at one end of my case, but to have it at both ends

is too confusing…' actually comes from 'The Adventure of the Illustrious Client'). Sherlock Holmes decides to dress up like a cleric then falsify a fire in order to trick

Miss Adler into revealing the photo's location… So far so alike. The nakedness and whipping are, however, all down to Steven Moffat, who was inspired by the fact that Irene Adler, 'of questionable and dubious memory', was always thought of as 'the Woman' that beat Sherlock Holmes. That she does so with a riding crop is all the more fun. ■

The Adventure of the Cheap Flat

You might think, after reading of Sherlock's exploits in the newspapers, that he works from a large office. A gleaming thing of filing cabinets, high-speed internet and large glass desks. He doesn't. He works from a flat decorated entirely in Lunatic Fungal Chic.

If the occasional pile of clutter offends you, by all means move it.

Last time I tried that I was bitten by a large spider you appeared to be using as a bookmark

A product of an early case. I call it Billy. When Mrs Hudson has seen fit not to try and throw it away. Again.

She says it's against Health and Safety.

Rubbish, it's probably the least dangerous of my ornaments. I think she uses it to give her soup flavour.

Probably the most violent way of keeping one's correspondence filed. →

Think yourself lucky I stick the knife in the letters not their authors.

← Sherlock prefers not to use the kitchen as it was originally intended. He'd rather fill it with poisonous gas and the odd explosion.

Well, what would you use it for?

The preparation of food, Sherlock. You know, FOOD. The solid stuff that goes into your mouth on the odd occasion it's not busy saying something clever.

The Adventure of the Cheap Flat

Sherlock is alarmingly well read.

Nothing alarming about it.

'The Stray Animal Cook book' by Alfred Blighj 'An illustrated Guide to Human Decomposition' by Warren Court; 'How to Kill a Man With Cutlery' by Shelley von Trampp. I stick by the word 'alarmingly'.

After a hard day reading up on decomposition, there's nothing Sherlock likes to do more than curl up with a copy of My Weekly.

All of life can be found in the personal columns of women's magazines.

'My Mental Flatmate Made My Life Hell!'

Never let it be said that Sherlock troubles himself with such petty concerns as the security deposit. Note the bullet holes in the wall. You might not be able to see them as they're well hidden by the spray-painted smiley-face.

I may have made some alterations but she chose that wallpaper. As far as I'm concerned that's a fair trade.

I've never been sure whether this was a joke or an experiment. 'To test how unendurable Sherlock's music collection is post mortem', perhaps.

I never lose them.

And they smell of antique antelope! Will the pleasures never end?

But Sherlock's an art lover too! See the inspiring 'Ammunition through the Ages', no doubt bought as a kindly Christmas present by his brother.

Much more of this and I'll test them on you.

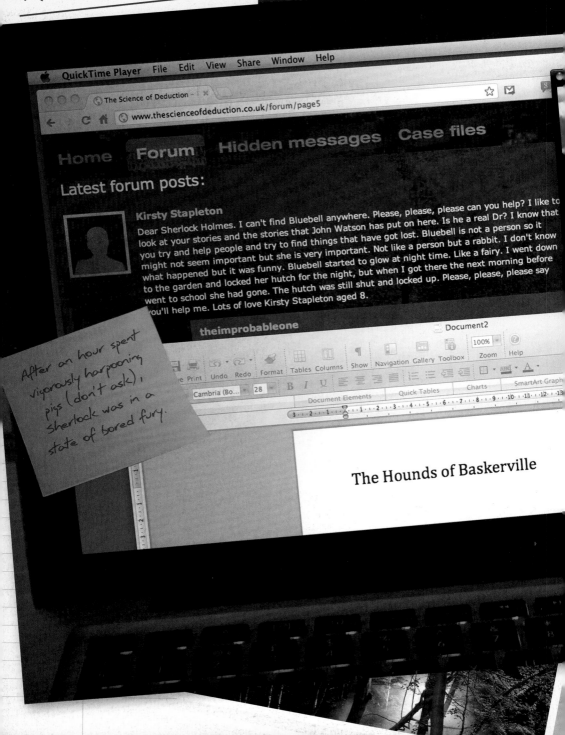

QuickTime Player   File   Edit   View   Share   Window   Help

The Science of Deduction –

www.thescienceofdeduction.co.uk/forum/page5

Home   **Forum**   **Hidden messages**   **Case files**

Latest forum posts:

Kirsty Stapleton

Dear Sherlock Holmes. I can't find Bluebell anywhere. Please, please, please can you help? I like to look at your stories and the stories that John Watson has put on here. Is he a real Dr? I know that you try and help people and try to find things that have got lost. Bluebell is not a person so it might not seem important but she is very important. Not like a person but a rabbit. I don't know what happened but it was funny. Bluebell started to glow at night time. Like a fairy. I went down to the garden and locked her hutch for the night, but when I got there the next morning before went to school she had gone. The hutch was still shut and locked up. Please, please, please say you'll help me. Lots of love Kirsty Stapleton aged 8.

theimprobableone   Document2

After an hour spent vigorously harpooning pigs (don't ask), Sherlock was in a state of bored fury.

Cambria (Bo...   28   B I U

The Hounds of Baskerville

THE BASKERVILLE MUTATIONS!

Since the end of the Second World War, Baskerville army base has been one of the country's most well-guarded secrets. The work that goes on there – investigating chemical and biological weapons projects – has been frequently debated in the press with many animal rights organisations claiming it is a hive of unethical and illegal experimentation. Claims that have been stringently denied by authorities. But we at THE TRUTH know better!

Last month I was able to talk to Henry Knight, a local man who has compelling evidence backing the claims that Baskerville has been breeding mutations for war. Mutations that have escaped.

'When I was a kid,' says Knight, 'my father and I used to go on walks up to Dewer's Hollow ['Dewer' is an ancient name for the devil as readers will remember from our analysis of the Hobb's Lane Mystery in Issue 28]. Since my mum had died, we used to spend a lot of time together and he was always telling me about the horrible things they were doing at the Baskerville centre. Then, one night, I saw it with my own eyes. Huge, with black fur and red eyes. It leaped on my father, dragging him screaming into the shadows. I was terrified. I mean, I was only seven, what could I do? I ran, God help me, I ran as that thing took my father…'

Luckily we had a visit from a man called Henry Knight to stop Sherlock destroying any more fixtures and fittings. Knight was haunted by a childhood memory of a terrible creature attacking his father, something his therapist, Dr Louise Mortimer, insisted was a fabricated memory covering up another trauma.

Sherlock agreed initially but was then fascinated when Knight explained that he had revisited Dewer's Hollow, the place where his father had gone missing, and found the footprints of a giant dog.

No, he said that 'They were the footprints of a gigantic hound.'

Why did he use such an archaic word?

Seven year-old Henry's drawing of what he thinks he saw.

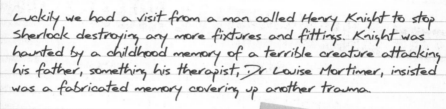

The Hounds of Baskerville

So off we went to Dartmoor. A train to Exeter and then a terrifying journey in a hired jeep to Grimpen village.

Terrifying? We survived, didn't we?

Just.

You're incredible. A genius. A good friend. And a lousy driver.

Tagged by John Watson:
Sherlock trying to impress some rocks by looking all moody.

Well, I get annoyed with all the gears.

All?
You only tried first.

Sa

From

To

Class Ticket type   Adult Child
STD SAVER RETURN   ONE   NIL
        Start date   Number
        30·JUN·11   28767 208
From   Valid until
LONDON TERMINALS   30·JUN·11
To   Route   Validity
EXETER ST DAVIDS ANY PERMITTED   SEE RESTRICTNS
                          2-PART RETURN

Tagged by John Watson:
Baskerville base on the right, Dewer's Hollow on the left. In between? A bloody minefield. The Great Grimpen Minefield in fact, reputed to contain more experimental weaponry than some small countries. All in all, a perfect holiday spot. Actually, for Sherlock it probably was.

Boutique Rooms
&
Vegetarian
Cuisine

Tagged by John Watson:
We found a place to stay, whose advertised vegetarian menu didn't seem to gel with a receipt I spotted on the bar.

It was too green. And there were cows. Loose. The country is hell.

Class · Ticket type
STD SAVER RETL

From
LONDON TERMINALS
To
EXETER ST DAVIDS

Start d.
30-JUN-11
Val.
30-J

Inv

ndershaw Meat Supplies

Cross Keys

V.A.T. Regd No.

070

The Hounds of Baskerville

Thanks to Gary and Billy, our landlords, we were pointed towards a local lad, Fletcher, who claimed to have seen the creature at Dewer's Hollow. In fact he claimed it to anyone who paid him £8.50 to go on his 'Walk in the Footsteps of the Beast' walking tour.

Well, he needed to feed his gambling habit somehow.

BEWARE THE HOUND!!

Sherlock convinced Fletcher that he had bet me fifty quid that he couldn't prove he'd seen the creature. After some theatrical spiel and a photo on his phone that could have been a distant terrier, he managed to offer some evidence.

As Sherlock would put it: the footprint of a gigantic hound.

Sherlock then decided we should take a look at Baskerville.
The surrounding area made their feelings towards visitors clear.

So, obviously, Sherlock decided
we should drive
straight in.

AUTHORISED PERSONNEL O
YOU ARE NOW ENTERING A RESTRICTED A

BASKERVILLE

THIS ESTABLISHMENT IS A PROHIBITED PLACE UNDER THE OFFICIAL SECRETS

NAME:
MYCROFT HOLMES
ID REF:
> > > > > 36409 93740
CLEARANCE LEVEL:
UNLIMITED
SIGNATURE:

We managed, thanks to
ID stolen from Mycroft, to
get into the place – and it
was nearly twenty minutes
until we were thrown out.
During which time Sherlock
managed to investigate the
disappearance of a rabbit
called Bluebell. Obviously
I was glad we were there
for such a good cause. The
case had come through to
Sherlock's website, sent by
Kirsty, the rabbit's young
owner.

Coincidence
is the crack
cocaine of
existence.

And the bane
of a detective's
life, I'd have
thought.

BLUEBELL

Not this
one.

We met Dr Stapleton, mother of Kirsty, and Sherlock managed to set her right at ease by accusing her of genetically modifying her daughter's pet rabbit. This was around the time we were thrown out of the building by Major Barrymore, the commanding officer.

We also met Dr Frankland, another scientist working there who helped to sneak us off site without bullets in our back. He was friends with Henry Knight's father and SHERLOCK'S GREATEST FAN.

You're just jealous because I have fans.

I have fans. There's a whole Tumblr blog dedicated to me. Run by Watson's Wenches.

Wenches? Plural? Are you sure?

The Hounds of Baskerville

We went to see our (incredibly rich) client. He had been visualising two words during therapy, 'Liberty' and 'In'. Sherlock explained his plan of action: take him out onto the moors at night and see if something ate him. Not Sherlock at his subtlest.

Needless to say, this plan was met with some nervousness on the part of Henry Knight.

Henry Knight is nervous of everything. He opens a coffee jar as if something might leap out at him.

As night fell, I spotted someone signalling in Morse code. I wrote down the message.

I told Sherlock about it but he and Knight were a little more interested in the gigantic hound they had just seen (though it took Sherlock ages to admit he'd seen a damn thing).

I had a row with Sherlock.

U M Q

R A

U M Q R A? That was the signal? What did the clue lead to?

Did you? Sorry, I must have missed that.

Nothing. Absolutely nothing. At all.

But he soon got round me by texting pictures of brunettes. Louise Mortimer to be precise, Knight's therapist. She was in the pub and he wanted me to try and get information out of her.

I failed miserably. Thanks to Bob Frankland dropping by the pub table and blowing my whole 'old friend of Henry's' disguise.

A double shame as not only was she very nice but I was beginning to think that Sherlock might benefit from her services. He was behaving even more strangely than usual.

H.O.U.N.D.

There was nothing wrong with me.

I was just trying to deduce how I could have seen a monstrous dog when, obviously, that was impossible.

But it began to look like it wasn't impossible after all.

Mycroft had sent Lestrade down to join us, which wound Sherlock up but was pretty useful when it came to getting to the bottom of the meat receipts in our 'vegetarian' hotel.

Sales Invoice

Undershaw

Sales Invoice

Sales Invoice

Undershaw M

Keys

It didn't take long for our landlords to admit that they'd bought a big dog in the hope of feeding the rumours and drumming up trade. They'd kept the dog in an old mineshaft on the moor but hadn't been able to control it so they'd had it put down. In the meantime, though, could it have been what Henry Knight and Sherlock saw?

Sherlock managed to negotiate with his brother to gain access to Baskerville in order to test a theory. We had 24 hours. Major Barrymore didn't like it but his hands were tied.

Sherlock wanted me to investigate the labs, Stapleton's in particular.

I began to explore, stepped into Stapleton's lab and then...

Not unless Pets R Us have started stocking dogs the size of pit ponies with glowing red eyes, no.

The Hounds of Baskerville

It was not
my proudest
moment.

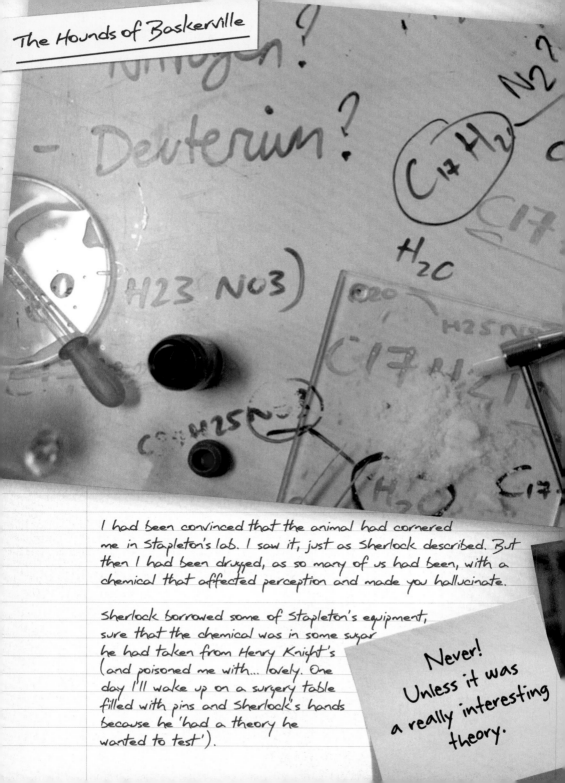

Nitrogen?

Deuterium?

N2?

$C_{17}H_2$

$C17$

$H23NO3)$

H_2O

$H2SN$

$C_{17}H_2$

C_{17}

$C_{17}H2SN$

(H_2O)

I had been convinced that the animal had cornered me in Stapleton's lab. I saw it, just as Sherlock described. But then I had been drugged, as so many of us had been, with a chemical that affected perception and made you hallucinate.

Sherlock borrowed some of Stapleton's equipment, sure that the chemical was in some sugar he had taken from Henry Knight's (and poisoned me with... lovely. One day I'll wake up on a surgery table filled with pins and Sherlock's hands because he 'had a theory he wanted to test').

Never!
Unless it was a really interesting theory.

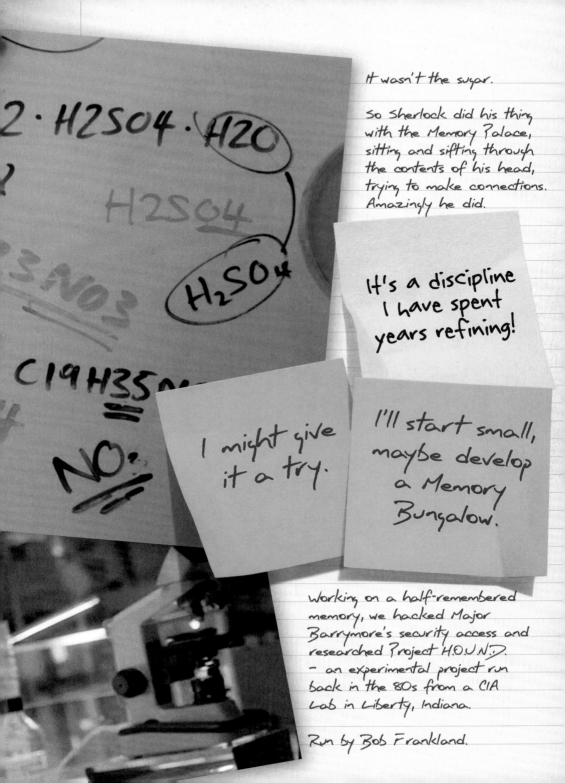

The project had been to develop an airborne deliriant as an anti-personnel weapon. But long-term exposure to the chemical had driven the test subjects mad. They became violent, dangerous, fear-stricken.

Just like Henry Knight who, according to Louise Mortimer, had just taken a few pot-shots at her with a handgun then gone running onto the moor.

We cornered Henry on the moor and managed to stop him hurting himself. Then Frankland arrived. Then the dog that Billy and Gary hadn't put down after all also arrived. Sherlock was REALLY enjoying himself by this point. Lestrade and I were far too busy trying to shoot a deranged, violent dog to see the fun side.

PAST T
CAN C
THIS A
THE O

The poison was in the fog all around us. We were hallucinating just as Henry had done on the night when Frankland had killed his father. Knight knew the work Frankland was doing and had threatened to expose him. So he had ended up experiencing that work first hand.

Frankland ran but entered the minefield and, within moments, the night sky was lit up by an explosion.

And that, officer, is what we did during our summer holidays...

THE ADVENTURE OF THE GIGANTIC HOUND

T *he Hound of the Baskervilles* is by far the most well-known Sherlock Holmes story. Conan Doyle wrote the novel a few years after killing off his detective but, having had the idea of a creepy tale set on Dartmoor, he soon realised that he needed a character like Holmes to make it work. Why create someone new when he had the man himself? The fact that readers were still clamouring for the return of Holmes can't have harmed the proposition either. Over the years, there have been twenty-four different adaptations, from 1914's silent German picture *Der Hund von Baskerville* to a recent adaptation by the BBC featuring the Australian Richard Roxburgh as Holmes. In between, we have had everything from animated versions (voiced by Peter O'Toole) to a bizarre 1978 spoof starring Peter Cook and Dudley Moore.

So, what does it matter if we have one more?

'There was a greater responsibility,' says Mark Gatiss, the writer of the episode, 'as there are so many famous elements to the story that people will expect to see. It was so difficult. I started saying, "It's not a hound, it's a bitch!"'

Mark's favourite adaptation was the 1959 version mounted by Hammer Studios featuring Peter Cushing as Holmes and Andre Morell as Dr Watson. Given his love for horror, it's not a surprising choice – the studio, having

Cushing and Morell investigate the Hound

achieved great success with a string of X-rated movies, went out of their way to try and make the story even more horrible so as to earn the all-important certificate. As it was, they only managed to earn an A (for adult) rating. Given how easily the subject matter lends itself to the grotesque, one can only imagine they weren't trying hard enough.

'It's the closest Sherlock Holmes gets to horror,' Mark agrees, 'though slightly hamstrung by the fact that it needs to present a rational explanation.'

And therein lies one of the trickiest problems of the story…

'The dog is always disappointing!' laughs Mark. 'Everyone always struggles when it comes to tackling the dog!'

Deciding that the modern-day equivalent of the ghost story would be a conspiracy theory, the fear of the scientific unknown, the Powers That Be and their diabolical plots, Mark transposed the original setting from dark, Gothic mansion to army base. Baskerville has become a research and development centre like Porton Down, a place where weapons come in test tubes and monsters are bred in underground laboratories.

Sidney Paget's interpretation of this classic tale

Another major change can be found in the length of time Sherlock appears in the story. Clearly showing how disinvested Doyle was in the character, Holmes is absent for a great deal of the original story, with Watson bearing the lion's share of the investigation. *The Hounds of Baskerville* acknowledges this for a moment when it appears that Holmes intends to send Watson to Dartmoor on his own.

'The thing is,' Mark explained to journalist Morgan Jeffery, 'the best way to do it is to grab it by the throat and treat it as a joke… You tip your hat to the original and then just say, "No, he's going to be in this one!"' ■

The monster as seen by Henry Knight

THE HOUNDS OF BASKERVILLE
BY THE BOOK

A GIGANTIC HOUND

Like *A Scandal in Belgravia*, *The Hounds of Baskerville* is filled with elements of the original, all slightly skewed so as to bring them up to date. Mark Gatiss even finds a way to keep the immortal line 'they were the footprints of a gigantic hound!' and make the archaic phraseology part of the plot.

THE LOSS OF A KNIGHTHOOD

In the original novel, the potential victim is Sir Henry

Baskerville. Russell Tovey's Henry Knight, the character's modern-day equivalent, has lost his title but retained reference to it in his surname.

THE TRUTH

One of Holmes's most famous quotes is 'When you have eliminated the impossible, whatever remains, however improbable, must be the truth.' Originally uttered in the second Holmes novel, *A Sign of Four*, it finds its modern home here, slightly rephrased.

OH, MR SELDEN!

In the novel, Barrymore is the butler at Baskerville Hall and he is caught by Watson signalling to his wife's brother with a lantern.

The brother Henry Selden, was an escaped convict from Dartmoor prison. He was also a whopping red herring.

Mark Gatiss retains the glimpsed flashing of a light on the moor, but the source is revealed as a selection of cars rocking in the darkness, with the breathless admission that 'Mr Selden, you've done it again.' Quite what Mr Selden has done, and how it may affect the insurance value of the vehicle, is left to the viewer's imagination. The fact that such car-based al-

fresco exploration is known as 'dogging' helps keep everything nicely on theme.

A CONDUCTOR OF LIGHT The novel opens with Holmes examining a walking cane left by a potential client. He asks Watson to try his hand at duplicating his methods (much as Sherlock does to John when analysing the trainers in *The Great Game*). When Watson has done so – and missed virtually everything of importance – Holmes says:

'Really, Watson, you excel yourself... I am bound to say that in all the accounts which you have been so good as to give of my own small achievements you have habitually underrated your own abilities. It may be that you are not yourself luminous, but you are a conductor of light. Some people

without possessing genius have a remarkable power of stimulating it. I confess, my dear fellow, that I am very much in your debt.'

The latter part of which, possibly the most anaemic compliment in literature, finds its way, rephrased, into this episode. ■

THE ADVENTURE
OF THE DIFFERING
DEERSTALKERS

THE HOLLYWOOD QUICKIE While Holmes has been seen in many guises on the silver screen, the fourteen movies made between 1939 and 1946 featuring Basil Rathbone as Holmes and Nigel Bruce as Watson are particularly well-remembered.

'Cheaply made but handsomely mounted,' says Mark Gatiss, 'offering genuine sincerity and pleasure. They're closer to the spirit of the original adventures, the ideas of those stories, than most other adaptations.'

Initially, an adaptation of Doyle's novel *The Hound of the Baskervilles* was presented by Twentieth Century Fox. It was a wonderfully Gothic piece that sat comfortably with the

horror output of the time – indeed, the same year saw Rathbone appear in one of Universal's Frankenstein sequels playing the son of the misguided scientist. *The Hound of the Baskervilles* was intended as a one-off production. Rathbone had primarily become known for playing villains and was deemed a lesser box-office draw than Richard Greene (cast as Sir Henry Baskerville), who received top-billing. Nigel Bruce fared even worse, appearing fourth on the poster beneath the movie's love interest Wendy Barrie. The film's immediate critical success and the clear on-screen chemistry between Rathbone and Bruce pointed the way forward, and Fox immediately rushed a sequel into production, the two stars now given pride of place on the movie's promotional material.

The Adventures of Sherlock Holmes, a melting pot of various plots and ideas that was more of a light-hearted romp than its predecessor, also fared well. George Zucco, a man who would become a familiar face to horror lovers throughout the 1940s, appeared as Professor Moriarty.

Despite the film's success, Fox decided not to make any more Holmes movies, but Universal Pictures revived the series in 1942. Universal saw the Sherlock Holmes stories as perfect material for a run of B-movies – cheap, quickly produced features designed to fill out the then

The legendary Basil Rathbone as Holmes

Another case for Holmes and Watson as the duo investigate *Terror By Night*...

common double-bill presentations in cinemas. Buying the rights to the character from the estate of Conan Doyle, they kept Rathbone and Bruce in their roles, as well as Mary Gordon as Mrs Hudson.

The one thing Universal had no interest in keeping was the historical setting of the previous movies. In 1942's *Sherlock Holmes and the Voice of Terror*, audiences instead met a present-day Holmes and Watson, battling Nazis in a plot that owed a great deal to the real-life and contemporaneous German propaganda broadcasts of 'Lord Haw-Haw'. Three more pictures followed in 1943: *Sherlock Holmes and the Secret Weapon*, *Sherlock Holmes in Washington* and *Sherlock Holmes Faces Death*. The latter saw Holmes and Watson set their sights further afield than Nazis, and the more general tone

continued in 1944 with the intrepid pair facing *The Spider Woman*, *The Scarlet Claw* and *The Pearl of Death*. *The Spider Woman* is a particular favourite of the *Sherlock* creators.

'It's the quintessential Holmes movie,' says Steven Moffat, 'with more plot than any other film.'

'Fifty-nine of the best minutes ever,' Mark agrees, noting the movie's short running time, not uncommon for a B-movie of the day.

'Genuinely muscular, pacey storytelling,' says Steven. 'Ten minutes in and you think, "Everything has now happened, there can be no more events!"'

The House of Fear, *The Woman in Green* and *Pursuit to Algiers* followed in 1945, with two more movies, *Terror by Night* and *Dressed to Kill* finishing the series the following year.

Fourteen movies in all, with twelve of those being produced over only five years, they did a great deal to cement Holmes and Watson as true icons in the mind of the public. Though the scripts varied in their connection with the original stories, with some utilising plot elements and others not bothering at all, the central relationship struck a chord and, for many, Rathbone and Bruce were *the* Holmes and Watson. Indeed, while the reviews for *Sherlock* have been universally positive, the spectre of Rathbone and Bruce even loomed over the response to the first episode, fifty-three years later:

'There was one review that made a fuss about the present-day setting,' explains Mark, 'saying, "This isn't proper Sherlock Holmes, he should be Victorian, go back and watch Basil Rathbone!" I nearly emailed to wish him luck, having only two out of the fourteen movies to choose from. Luckily someone else got there before me!'

THE PRIVATE LIFE

Released in 1970, *The Private Life of Sherlock Holmes* was a somewhat beleaguered production that has nonetheless become a cult classic.

Since the 1950s, American studios were keen to lure audiences away from television screens and into movie theatres. One method was the roadshow picture, an unusually long feature, often screened with an intermission, that could play to select theatres before going on general release (often in a trimmed version). These epics, from sword-and-sandal classics such as *Ben Hur* (1959) and *Spartacus* (1960) to the machine-gun-wielding *Where Eagles Dare* (1968) or the brain food of Stanley Kubrick's *2001 – A Space Odyssey* (1968), often took advantage of widescreen ratios and the increased quality of stereo sound to offer big visual experiences, huge cinematic vistas and sweeping soundtracks. Billy Wilder's *The Private Life of Sherlock Holmes* was destined to be released in the same manner but an increasing caution on the part of movie studios, bitten by recent costly failures, and the disillusionment of the director himself, saw the film heavily cut.

Wilder had established his credentials in the 1940s as a director of film noirs such as *Double Indemnity* (1944) and *Sunset Boulevard* (1950). He went on to become famous for a string of comedy movies including the sublime *Some Like it Hot* (1959). Sadly, by the late 1960s, his career was foundering and the negative experience of his Holmes movie hardly helped.

The Private Life of Sherlock Holmes featured Robert Stephens as Holmes and Colin Blakely as Watson.

Robert Stephens and Colin Blakely as Billy Wilder's Holmes and Watson

Christopher Lee's Mycroft – inspiration for *Sherlock*

Originally intended to offer four separate stories, the final cut was reduced to two: a light-hearted tale of Holmes avoiding the attentions of a Russian ballet dancer by insisting he's gay (and in a relationship with Watson), and a Boy's Own adventure involving spies, submarines and Loch Ness.

Extra material was shot, including a vignette of Holmes during his university days, a separate introduction and a bizarre murder in an upside-down room, but while some material has found its way onto commercial releases as bonus features, the cinematic cut, running at a shade over two hours, is the version we are left with. It's important to note that Wilder cut the film himself, not the studio; he was as uncertain of the intended three-hour cut as anyone else and made the choice independent of executive interference.

Though it may sound as if it offers a somewhat absurd view of our detective and his friend, the movie has long been a firm favourite amongst fans of Sherlock Holmes. Like the Rathbone pictures before it, it gets to the heart of these two characters and was a huge influence on the production of *Sherlock*.

'Our Mycroft is not Doyle's,' admits Mark Gatiss, 'but Billy Wilder's.' Hugely fat in the books, Mycroft is here played by Christopher Lee as a wiry, Machiavellian character. The Diogenes Club – established in Doyle's tales by Mycroft as a place to hold all the 'most un-clubbable men in London' – has become nothing more than a front for the British Secret Service. 'A wonderful idea,' enthuses Steven Moffat. And one frequently nicked by writers of pastiche Sherlock Holmes adventures ever since.

'It's a fabulously melancholy movie,' says Mark. 'Funny, irreverent and yet somehow very, very reverent.'

Sadly a failure at the box office, it has now taken on a life of its own on home video and is frequently cited as one of the best big-screen versions of Holmes.

THE LABOUR OF LOVE For many years, despite so many other actors appearing in the roles, the image of Holmes and Watson was irrevocably linked with Basil Rathbone and Nigel Bruce. That began to change in 1984, with the production of a brand new series of adaptations by Granada Television for ITV. Jeremy Brett was cast as Holmes, and he brought a passion and determination to the role that frequently had the sides of your television set expanding. Determined to be the best, most accurate screen Holmes ever seen – a notion brought out of obsession rather than arrogance – Brett compiled exhaustive notes on the character and lived the part with a ferocity that was perhaps not altogether healthy.

Brett had long been friends with Robert Stephens. Knowing Brett's mental state, and with his own experience in *The Private Life of Sherlock Holmes*, Stephens tried to persuade him not to take the part. 'I was lucky it didn't kill me,' he told Brett. 'You will have to go into such a pit to get into that man that you will self-destruct.'

Brett was diagnosed with manic depression in 1986, and he spent the rest of his years in the role becoming more and more unwell. He was prescribed Lithium tablets for his depression which took their toll, causing fluid retention, muddling his thoughts and damaging his heart. He was also a match for his character in the art of consuming tobacco, reportedly smoking upwards of sixty cigarettes a day. His manic episodes

Jeremy Brett and David Burke take up the mantle of Holmes and Watson

Jeremy Brett immersed himself in the role of Sherlock Holmes for ten years

continued, varying in severity but peaking with an attack that saw him found on Clapham Common, near his home, with bleeding, bare feet, lost in conversation with an imaginary figure. 'I am trying,' he later told his partner Linda Pritchard, 'I am bloody well trying to shake him off, but Holmes seems to haunt me these days.' Perhaps Robert Stephens had been right.

Towards the end of his run in the part, Brett was struggling to read his scripts and constantly attended on by Linda. That he still managed to excel in the role is testament to his skill, though one episode of the last filmed series featured Charles Gray as Mycroft Holmes filling in for his fictional brother as Brett simply couldn't manage to film.

The decline in Brett's health should not overshadow what was a masterful run of adaptations, however. John Watson was originally played by David Burke, with Edward Hardwicke taking over the role after two series. Between them, they provided yet another landmark take on Sir Arthur Conan Doyle's characters and for many became the definitive actors in the roles, though Brett himself didn't agree. 'To me,' he said during his final promotional tour for the show in 1995, 'Basil Rathbone is You Know Who.' By that point he wouldn't even refer to the character by name.

The series came to an end in 1994, having totalled thirty-six 50-minute episodes as well as five feature-length specials. Brett died the following year. ■

Reichenbach Fall

When I started putting these pieces together, gathering the evidence, the notes, the clippings, I did it because I was proud. Proud to have been involved. Proud to have known the man who was responsible for each and every pixel, scribble or bit of newsprint. I thought maybe they'd help me, I don't know, build something. Work them together into something more. A book maybe.

I know he didn't approve. He made his opinion clear on each and every page. Well, no, that's not altogether true, he didn't mind as much as he made out. If there was one thing he always liked it was attention.

But I don't think they're a book. Not any more.

These scraps of information are pieces of a life, a window into the time I spent with the most remarkable human being I have ever known. My friend. My best friend. Sherlock Holmes.

They are a memorial.

And this is the epitaph. The notes that led up to his fall.

Our final problem.

The Reichenbach Fall

It started with me suggesting Sherlock lower his profile a bit.
After the success of the Reichenbach case, we had been getting
far too much attention, and it was only a matter of time
before the press turned. Because that's just what journalists do,
they build people up and then tear them down.

But then came Moriarty.

CRIME OF THE CENTURY?

By **Aileen Hickey** Crime Correspondent

QUESTIONS are being asked in parliament as to how the Tower of London, Pentonville Prison and the Bank of England were all broken into at the same time by the same man – James Moriarty.

There are unconfirmed reports that Scotland Yard's favourite sleuth Mr Sherlock Holmes has been called in to help the team piece together the most audacious crime

TURN TO PAGE 5

Scotland Yard calls upon 'nation's favourite detective' in Moriarty trail

Janette Owen

In a twist worthy of a Conan Doyle novella, Mr Sherlock Holmes was yesterday revealed to be an expert witness at the trial of 'Jim' Moriarty. Described by many commentators as the trial of the century, the case has all the ingredients of a block buster film. The royal family, Scotland yard, the world of finance and greed, the 'underclass' of prisoners out to reek revenge as they enjoy their own fifteen minutes of freedom. The case is riddled with irony and intrigue but perhaps reflects a deeper malaise that seems to be at the heart of a society.

Mr Holmes, a man of few words, declined to comment when asked about his involvement in the case. It is understood that a woefully depleted Scotland

Despite my best attempts to coach him in the art of not showing off in public, Sherlock's appearance in the witness stand did not go well.

But while that was no great surprise, the verdict certainly was. Moriarty had offered no evidence to support his not-guilty plea and yet...

Expert Witness Charged With Contempt

Today, at the Moriarty Trial, expert witness and well-known detective Mr Sherlock Holmes turned on the judge and found himself on the wrong side of the dock!

When asked to describe the accused, Mr Holmes said: 'James Moriarty isn't a man at all. He's a spider. A spider at the centre of a web, a criminal web precisely how each and every one of them dances.'

Mr Holmes then proceeded to lecture the prosecuting counsel about their jobs before, in response to a dressing down from the Judge, describing, in brutal detail, the Right Honourable gentlemen's bedroom habits and how they involved the clerk of the court, Mr Lionel Forrester. ●

Moriarty paid one final visit to Sherlock, crowing about the technology he possessed that had allowed him to break into three of the most secure buildings in the country. He had a key, a couple of lines of computer code, that meant he could crack anything: open doors, empty bank accounts, fire missiles...

But really, all he wanted to do was break Sherlock.

MORIARTY WALKS FREE

Shock verdict at ~~S~~ ~~ey~~ trial

30p

SHERLOCK: THE SHOCKING TRUTH

(Close friend Richard Brook Tells All)

EXCLUSIVE

Exclusive from Kitty Reilly

SUPER-SLEUTH Sherlock Holmes has today been exposed as a fraud in a revelation that will shock his new-found horde of fans.

Out of work actor Richard Brook revealed exclusively to THE SUN that he was hired by Holmes in an elaborate deception to fool the British public into

believing that Holmes had 'above-average detective skills'.

Brook, who has known Holmes for decades and until ...

10p DA

The Reichenbach Fall

As if the newspaper backlash wasn't enough, Mycroft decided to warn me about some of our new neighbours.

Sulejmani, a member of an Albanian hit squad, currently living two doors away.

Ludmilla Dyachenko, Russian killer, now in flat opposite.

Stefan Tribek, Eastern-European assassin, just started working at computer repair shop at the end of the street.

Jaume Gauss, Bolivian sniper, renting top-floor flat across the road.

Mycroft wanted me to look out for Sherlock. To keep him safe. I tried.

Returning to Baker Street, I found a small brown envelope, sealed with wax, containing nothing but breadcrumbs. I had no idea what it could mean and, before I could ask Sherlock, we were whisked away on another case by Lestrade: the St Aldates School kidnapping.

Max and Claudette Bruhl, seven and nine respectively, the children of Rufus Bruhl, ambassador to the US. The ambassador had requested Sherlock specifically.

ST ALDATES

prospectus

BOARDING SCHOOL

KLETON, SURREY

The Reichenbach Fall

Sherlock analysed the boy's room first, coming to the conclusion that - in the few seconds before seeing someone coming for him through the glass of the door and being grabbed - he would have left a message. A call to Anderson and he was proven right.

The note was written in linseed oil, the closest thing Max Bruhl had to hand, having prepared his cricket bat with it earlier.

The boy had walked in the oil, leaving a short trail that showed us how he and his sister had been dragged out into the corridor.

Convinced that Moriarty was behind the abduction, Sherlock took a sample of the oil left by the killer's shoe and analysed it.

1. CHALK
2. ASPHALT
3. BRICK DUST
4. VEGETATION
5. ?????

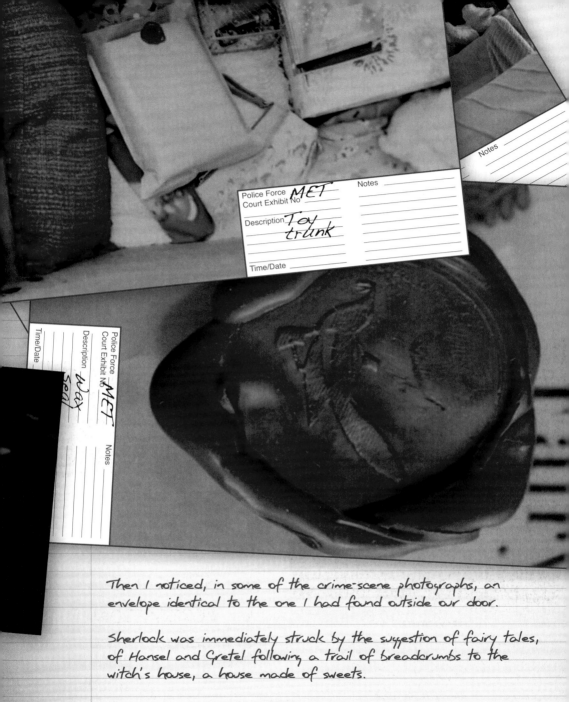

Police Force _MET_
Court Exhibit No
Description _Toy trunk_

Notes _____

Time/Date _____

Police Force _MET_
Court Exhibit No
Description _Wax seal_
Time/Date
Notes

Then I noticed, in some of the crime-scene photographs, an envelope identical to the one I had found outside our door.

Sherlock was immediately struck by the suggestion of fairy tales, of Hansel and Gretel following a trail of breadcrumbs to the witch's house, a house made of sweets.

The missing component of his analysis, the glycerol molecule found in the tread of the kidnapper's shoe, was ?G?R, used in the manufacture of chocolate.

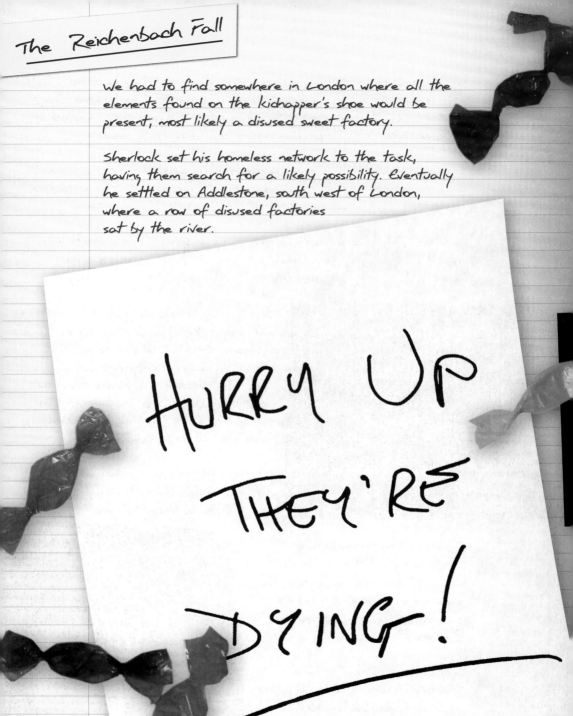

The Reichenbach Fall

We had to find somewhere in London where all the elements found on the kidnapper's shoe would be present, most likely a disused sweet factory.

Sherlock set his homeless network to the task, having them search for a likely possibility. Eventually he settled on Addlestone, south west of London, where a row of disused factories sat by the river.

HURRY UP THEY'RE DYING!

We found them, terrified, hiding in the shadows. They had been left with nothing to eat but mercury-laced chocolates. The hungrier they got the more they ate, and the more of the poison they ingested. If we had taken any longer they would certainly have died.

Sherlock tried to ask Claudette Bruhl some questions, but the moment she saw him she began to scream. It was this, this master stroke on Moriarty's part, that began to set Scotland Yard against him.

Lestrade had always been a lone voice in Sherlock's support. Nobody else liked him. But they tolerated him. Not any more. Now they began looking into the possbility that Sherlock was the kidnapper.

Sherlock returned to Baker Street with me following on behind. Wasn't I always, one way or the other? I didn't see what happened but Sherlock described it to me - a car nearly hit him but a man pulled him out of the way. That man had then been shot by an unseen sniper.

I recognised Sherlock's saviour from the photograph Mycroft had shown me: Sulejmani, the Albanian.

Sherlock was immediately convinced that the assassins were not here to harm him, they were here to protect him. He had something they all wanted. But what?

We searched the flat and Sherlock found a camera hidden on one of the bookshelves. We had been under surveillance for some time.

One more message from Moriarty, the Big Bad Fairy Tale villain and then the police were on our doorstep and I had a decision to make.

Grimm's Fairy

GENIUS DETECTIVE ON THE RUN

by **Aileen Hickey**
Crime Correspondant

In a shocking turn of events Mr Sherlock Holmes, the famed consulting detective, is now wanted by the very police force he often assisted.

Following his investigation of the Bruhl kidnapping, certain evidence has come to light that suggests he may have been in league with the kidnappers all along.

"It's always been suspicious," says a Scotland Yard insider, "how he seemed to know all the answers, well now we know. It's not difficult to solve the crimes if you planned them all in the first place."

This revelation comes at a time when another paper has also promised an exposé that claims to lift the lid on the relationship between Mr Holmes and James Moriarty, a man they claim is actually Rich Brook, an actor employed by Holmes to play the role of the master criminal.

Assault

Officers attended Mr Holmes's residence in Baker Street, wishing to take the man into custody. After initially accepting his arrest, Holmes then fled from the police in the company of his live-in colleague, John Watson. Watson, a confirmed bachelor, is said to have assaulted the Chief Constable during the arrest and, while Mr Holmes claimed the young doctor was his hostage, it is being assumed that he went willingly with his close friend.

I made my choice.

On the run, our first step was to interrogate one of the assassins that had been sent to watch over us. They were after the computer code, the key that Moriarty had used to break in to the Tower of London, Pentonville and the Bank of England. He had hidden it in our flat, his message to 'Get Sherlock' now all too clear.

But where was Moriarty? We decided to track down Kitty Reilly, the journalist offering the scoop on 'Richard Brook'.

And in doing so, bumped into the man himself, insisting that he was a creation of Sherlock's, that he was nothing more than a jobbing actor - ex of 'Emergency', the medical drama that wouldn't know a correct diagnosis if you forced one on it with a scalpel.

'Award Winning Actor Joins The Cast of Top

RICHARD BROOK
Curriculum Vitae

richard@r-brook.
Tel: 020 7946 0749
5 Cranston Hill,
London W1A 9C

About me

Height 5 feet 10 inches. Brown Eyes. Born 1976 Full Drivin
BADC intermediate certificate in Stage Fighting, Horse Riding, Woo
Leader, Chorus Dancing, Skiing, Tennis, Scuba Diving, Computing
Rich is best known for playing the heroic young anaesthetist Brian
the long-running BBC1 Medical Drama Emergency.

Education

BaHons	PERFORMING ARTS	
Foundation	PERFORMANCE	
A-level	DRAMA	
NOCN	PERFORMING ARTS	

Theatre Includes

_Long day's journey into night	Edmund	_National Theatre world tour
_As you like it	Touchstone	_RSC
_Great expectations	Narrator	_Liverpool playhouse
_The Importance of Being Ernest	Algie	_Yvonne Arnaud
_The Odyssey	Achilles	_Chichester
		_Royal Court upstairs

'New Face on the Emergency Ward'

Brian Stokes, new face on
'Emergency' ward, took tim
this week to talk to us ab
his demanding new
'Brian's a lot like me re
claimed the actor playing
- Rich Brook. 'He's a bit
rogue - a bit of a rebel
afraid to take a risk no
then.'

possession

'Hamlet for a New Generation'

It's taken almost two years of planning but finally Surbiton in Surrey
has its own civic theatre. And tonight the curtain will be raised on its
inaugural production - Shakespeare's 'Hamlet'. Directed by and starring
TV's Rich Brook - famous for his regular role in BBC 1's long running
Medical show 'Emergency' - Brook heads a cast of virtual unknowns..

Read more...

He had a great deal of evidence, CVs, press articles, DVDs...

But most of all he had threads of Sherlock's life, details
of his childhood, his growing up, things only a man that
really knew him could have known. Things that would make
people believe him.

Things he had learned from Mycroft.

Mycroft had been interrogating him for weeks, never able to
get more than a few worthless bits of information from him.
But Moriarty got so much more.

The Reichenbach Fall

And that is almost it. We were hiding at St Barts, not knowing what to do next, when I received a phone call from someone claiming to be from Scotland Yard. They told me Mrs Hudson had been shot. They told me she was dying. I argued with Sherlock when he refused to come with me. I said things to him that I wish I hadn't said. Because he knew. He always knows. It was a trick, there was nothing wrong with Mrs Hudson at all.

By the time I returned to the hospital he was on the roof. Sherlock. Standing on the edge. He called me. Tried to convince me that he was a fake. That everything they had said about him was true. I wouldn't believe it. I still won't. He was being forced to say it. Had to say it.

Then he jumped.

I owe him so much. I needed him. I still do.

But he's gone.

He told me once that I shouldn't make people into heroes. He said that heroes didn't exist and that even if they did he wouldn't be one of them.

Which goes to show. He wasn't always right about everything.

This book is published to accompany *Sherlock*, broadcast on BBC ONE.

Sherlock is a Hartswood Films production for BBC Cymru Wales,
co-produced with MASTERPIECE.

Executive Producers: Beryl Vertue, Mark Gatiss and Steven Moffat
Executive Producer for the BBC: Bethan Jones
Executive Producer for MASTERPIECE: Rebecca Eaton
Series Producer: Sue Vertue

10 9 8 7 6

Published in 2012 by BBC Books, an imprint of Ebury Publishing.
A Random House Group Company.

The Random House Group Limited Reg. No. 954009

Addresses for companies within the Random House Group
can be found at www.randomhouse.co.uk

A CIP catalogue record for this book is available from the British Library.

ISBN 978 1 849 90425 4

The Random House Group Limited supports The Forest Stewardship Council® (FSC®),
the leading international forest-certification organisation. Our books carrying the FSC
label are printed on FSC®-certified paper. FSC is the only forest-certification scheme
supported by the leading environmental organisations, including Greenpeace. Our paper
procurement policy can be found at www.randomhouse.co.uk/environment

MIX
Paper from
responsible sources
FSC www.fsc.org **FSC™ C004592**

Commissioning Editor: Albert DePetrillo
Project Editors: Steve Tribe & Laura Higginson
Design: Richard Atkinson

All images copyright © Hartswood Films
except: page 29 (bottom, thumbnails), 75, 83, 134, 140, 141,
142 and 143 © Rex Features; page 48 © Oxford University
Press, Penguin and Little Brown; page 50 © Geographers
A-Z Map Company; page 81 © New York Public Library;
page 81 (right, thumbnail) © Jonathan Cape; page 136
(top left, thumbnail) © Vintage Classics.

Colour origination by Altaimage, London. Printed and bound
by Firmengruppe APPL, aprinta druck, Wemding, Germany

To buy books by your favourite authors and register for offers,
visit www.randomhouse.co.uk

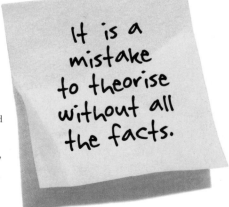

It is a mistake to theorise without all the facts.